how to really **parent** your child

Ross Campbell, M.D.
with Rob Suggs

W PUBLISHING GROUP™

www.wpublishinggroup.com

A Division of Thomas Nelson, Inc.
www.ThomasNelson.com

Published by W Publishing Group, a Division of Thomas Nelson, Inc., P.O. Box 141000, Nashville, Tennessee 37214.

W Publishing Group books may be purchased in bulk for educational, business, fundraising, or sales promotional use. For information, please e-mail SpecialMarkets@ThomasNelson.com.

Library of Congress Cataloging-in-Publication Data

Campbell, Ross, 1936–
   How to really parent your child / by Ross Campbell with Rob Suggs.
    p. cm.
   ISBN 0-8499-4541-0
   1. Parenting—Religious aspects—Christianity.   I. Suggs, Rob.
II. Title.
BV4529.C36   2005
248.8'45—dc22

                                         2004025673

Printed in the United States of America
05 06 07 08 RRD 6 5 4 3 2 1

how to really **parent** your child

CONTENTS

Contents

FOREWORD

Most parents sincerely hope that their children will grow up to be responsible adults. What many parents do not fully realize is that the manner in which a child is reared has a great deal to do with whether or not this wish becomes reality. In the cultural climate of the twenty-first century, it is even more difficult to be an effective parent. In the so-called Information Age, much of the information to which children are exposed runs counter to the biblical view of what makes a responsible adult. The pluralistic views expressed via television, movies, the Internet, and educational systems often bring confusion to young minds. More than ever, children need the sound guidance of mature parents.

The problem is that many parents were not parented well themselves, nor have they discovered positive principles of effective parenting. Even those who had wise parents are often confused in the midst of a changing culture. "Will the principles that my parents followed be effective with my own children?" is the question many parents are asking.

I know of no one more qualified to speak to concerned parents about effective parenting in the contemporary world than Dr. Ross Campbell, a psychiatrist with a Christian worldview, who has had over thirty years' experience working with children and their parents. In this book, *How to Really Parent Your Child,* Dr. Campbell helps parents learn to be proactive rather than reactive; to meet the child's needs rather than reacting to the child's behavior. He begins with the foundation stone: meeting the child's emotional need for love. In my own counseling practice, I have often encountered children who do not feel loved and parents who are frustrated because, in their minds, they have been loving the child since the child's birth. Parental sincerity is not enough; we must learn how to effectively fill a child's love tank. Parents inadvertently offer conditional love based on the child's behavior rather than unconditional love, which is what the child desperately needs. Dr. Campbell's practical approach to expressing unconditional love will help parents effectively love their children.

When the child feels secure in the parents' love, he or she is much more likely to receive discipline and instruction from the parent. Dr. Campbell points the way to loving discipline: acting in the child's best interest as opposed to reacting out of anger to the child's behavior. The parent who learns to give loving discipline is the parent who will effectively influence the child toward responsible behavior.

A common roadblock on the way to maturity is the mismanagement of anger. Parents are sometimes attempting to teach their children to handle anger in a responsible way, when

Foreword

they themselves have not learned to do so. The parent who is willing to be honest and sincerely wants to learn positive ways to handle anger will find this book a source of great help.

In spite of the harmful influences in contemporary culture, parents can effectively build positive character into the lives of their children. All of the research indicates that parents continue to have the greatest influence on the lives of their children. In fact, responsible parents largely determine the amount of time children spend watching movies, TV, video games, and computers. We cannot isolate our children from the changing culture, but we do have the responsibility to help them filter out those influences that would destroy their well-being.

Successful parenting requires information, motivation, and consistency. *How to Really Parent Your Child* will give you practical help in these three areas. Your dream of seeing your children become responsible adults can be a reality. If you are successful in the challenge of positive parenting, your child will reach his or her potential for good and God in the world. What could be more rewarding for a parent?

—Gary D. Chapman, Ph.D.
Author, *The Five Love Languages*
President, Marriage and Family Life Consultants, Inc.
Winston-Salem, North Carolina
GaryChapman.org

DARK CLOUDS . . .
WITH SILVER LININGS

THIS IS A BOOK OF GOOD NEWS FOR TOUGH TIMES.

As a loving and serious parent, you want to excel as a parent. You can envision that special day, years from now, when your children enter the world as confident, happy, and mature young adults—people of integrity who are eager to serve their Lord and their fellow human beings.

I need not tell you that we're living in a new world. As a matter of fact, this world is changing and evolving more rapidly than at any time in human history. Yes, there are some very dark and ominous clouds. In the introduction, we'll take a look at some of the particulars—an overview of these turbulent times.

But don't be discouraged, because the good news far overwhelms the bad. The good news is that it's just as possible as ever to be a terrific parent. Our culture may be deteriorating, but our God is still in control. And he wants to take your hand and walk beside you during these short, crucial years when your young ones look to you to teach them how to live.

If those clouds are darker, then the light entrusted to you shines even more brightly—the light of all the good and gracious things you're eager to bestow upon your children. If the world is lacking in integrity, how much more powerful your lessons in honesty and character will be. If our culture is obsessed with sex and violence, how much more appealing will be your guidance in the truth and goodness of the Christian alternative.

Therefore, this book is not about the despair of the clouds but about the hope of the silver lining: the good news that your parenting experience can and will be thrilling, fruitful, and deeply satisfying. No joy in life can surpass that of seeing your children become candles of hope in a dark world.

Follow the truth in these pages, and your success will be guaranteed. The chapters here represent the distillation of years of working with parents and their children, seeing the problems as well as the solutions. I've seen good things happen again and again, in hundreds of families who have faced these same challenges. My hope and my prayer are that your story will join or even exceed the stories of those who have come before you—achievers of distinction, overcomers in the art of good parenting.

—Ross Campbell

INTRODUCTION: LOST IN A STRANGE NEW WORLD

Dorothy and toto, her little dog, have been overtaken by a Kansas twister. Will the family home provide shelter from the storm?

The girl picks up the dog and rushes inside, just as the farmhouse is lifted into the air by the powerful gusts. The building begins a mad journey through the sky.

Dorothy gazes out the window helplessly as the cultural debris of her community is borne away by the angry wind. In some cases, the storm transforms the old and familiar into things new and frightening. A neighbor on her bicycle becomes a witch on a broom.

If you remember the film, you know what happens next. When the house settles to earth, Dorothy throws open the door to a world dazzlingly changed from the old-fashioned tones of black and white. Everything outdoors sparkles with bright candy colors. Nothing is the same.

"Toto," the girl whispers apprehensively to her terrier, "I don't think we're in Kansas anymore."

Dorothy is in a strange new world, and after a series of adventures with her new friends on the yellow brick road, she decides that there's no place like home, after all.

The heroine of *The Wizard of Oz* is right, of course: Home is the ultimate shelter, a refuge we should be able to depend on. The family is the foundation of our society, and it should be tough enough to withstand the winds of change.

Yet here in the early years of a new century, we find ourselves whirling through a turbulent atmosphere. We feel as lost and disoriented as Dorothy—this is not our parents' world. Their old-fashioned, black-and-white, small-town America is gone with the wind.

About one generation after Dorothy's cinematic fantasy journey, our culture entered its era of turmoil and transformation. The real upheaval began in the late 1960s, but the last decade has been particularly traumatic. As a matter of fact, when I retired from counseling in 1996, I believed my work as an author was done. Ever since then, I have seen the world around us spin even more out of control, offering challenges even greater than the ones we already faced. Those of us who are parents recognize the changes, but we need to recognize them fully and clearly.

The cultural tornado first broke loose in the late 1960s. The Vietnam era and the countercultural revolution finally climaxed with Watergate—a crisis of ethics and trust. We began to hear about the "generation gap" and its pessimism about communication between parents and their children.

Introduction

The commercial exploitation of cultural issues—music, movies, media, morals—exacerbated the problem and drove a painful wedge through families.

On a less sensational but equally influential level, the pervasive growth of the behavior modification mind-set took its toll. "Behavior mod" is the pragmatism-based strategy of altering someone's behavior by rewarding the desired responses and punishing the undesirable. In other words, when the lab rat taps the correct pedal, he is given his cheese; when he taps the wrong one, he receives a mild electric shock.

Many therapists, educators, parents, and authors made the mistake of assuming that what works for the lab rat is good for the human child. They forgot that while simple creatures respond effectively to deliberately inflicted pain, children will be damaged and resentful. Our kids are best molded by love, wisdom, and effective relational skills, with discipline in the right measure and at the right time.

PARENTS IN PANIC

The 1960s cultural explosion left families frightened and in some degree of panic. Our kids seemed to be running wild under the influence of sex, drugs, and rock-and-roll. It occurred to many that Dr. Benjamin Spock, with his anti-spanking policy, must have had everything wrong; surely we had spared the rod and spoiled the child.

So there was a predictable backlash, particularly in conservative and religious circles. Spanking was not only permissible but strongly advocated. I firmly believe that the mind-set of behavior modification, applied to the strategy of heavy-handed discipline, resulted in a lethal mix in our homes. As we will see in a later chapter, overly aggressive discipline (as a substitute for love and good communication) results in a slowly festering anger in our children. The anger boils like an unwatched pot until it spills over in every direction, causing pain for the child and everyone else.

It is my observation that we are reaping the harvest of a very angry generation. There is anger growing not only in our homes but throughout our stressful world—a world filled with violence including international terrorism, crowded classrooms and expressways, more and wider travel, a more hectic pace of life, greater choices and more danger, and a raw, rash, and rude pop culture. We have greater fears regarding conditions ranging from environmental deterioration to crime that is more pervasive and sophisticated.

I also see the issue of integrity looming larger than ever. Basic honesty and promise-keeping can no longer be taken for granted. As a nation we came to our nadir when an American president lied under oath. That sent a tragic message to a country already struggling with this issue. You can be certain that issues of integrity will impact your home and your children in ways you never anticipated. Will your kids tell the truth? Will they cheat on tests? Will they keep their commitments and live up to their responsibilities? These are basic values that were once culturally ingrained in each passing generation. In this new world, we find ourselves in an integrity crisis.

Meanwhile, all around us is the tornado whirl that perhaps defines our time more than any other: the unceasing whirl of information—information from the Internet, information from scientists, information on everything imaginable and too much of it for you and me to process. There is information available to your children that can damage their young souls at the tenderest and most fragile moments of their growth processes, and it is more and more difficult for parents to provide shelter from the storm of information.

What happens when we combine all the confusion, disorientation, and stress of "culture shock" with the loss of integrity and the seething power of anger that lie beneath the surface of many people's state of mind today? We reap the whirlwind.

This new world has come to be known by the label *postmodern*. C. Wright Mills foresaw the arrival of a postmodern world in 1959 in purely sociological terms. Our old industrial culture, he predicted, would shift to a clerical and service-oriented one. He saw such changes as the rise of multinational corporations and particularly the upheaval of the family. He wondered how the traditional family would survive or possibly evolve to some new form or forms.[1] He never took into consideration the additional factors we have considered: the Vietnam era, behavior modification, and imbalanced discipline.

Even so, we need to understand that this is indeed a new world. Its banners are pluralism, freedom of sensual expression, unease of spiritual expression, rampant consumerism, nearly unlimited mobility, and the ideal of perpetual entertainment. Our world wants us to accept the dictum that multiple beliefs imply multiple realities, none of which are necessarily rooted in ultimate truth—thus if your religion seems valid to you, it is only as true as any other religion. Faith becomes simply another consumer issue: We proceed to the religion store and select the most convenient set of beliefs—or even mix and match.

Edward Shorter, in his 1975 book *The Making of the Modern Family*, ventured an early portrait of the emerging postmodern family. He pointed to three new hallmarks: adolescent indifference to family identity, marital instability and divorce, and the loss of the "nest" concept of home with the advent of women's liberation.[2]

But few could have foreseen the effect of declining cultural values. Obviously, loosened sexual restrictions and drug abuse have taken their toll. But there have been subtler changes, too: Our very ideals have been remolded by the new world. Do you remember when our society's highest priorities were better citizenship and strong character development, rather than wealth and comfort? Do you remember when we worried about the growth of integrity and values in our children, rather than simply admittance to the most prestigious universities?

A recent Gallup poll indicated that the number one desire of most people was to be rich; number two was to be thin. In a world where many parents hold such mind-sets, how can we expect our children—the rising generation—to better manage a more complex and dangerous world?

Recently I was tidying up at home when I came across an unmarked videotape. I could tell the tape had been collecting dust for a good while, so I was curious to discover its contents. Into the VCR it went, and I sat down to watch what turned out to be a procession of old television situation comedies. Perhaps one of our kids had made the tape for later viewing. As I reviewed the shows, I was shocked by how much had changed between then and now. And what time period do you think I'm alluding to? The 1950s? The early 1960s? No, these shows were only seven years old. In that brief period, the networks had abandoned the approach of shows about families that taught helpful little lessons about life. The recorded shows mirrored a world of ethics and values.

Spend an evening in front of your television today and you won't come away with such a conclusion. Our shows are "shows about nothing," as a recent hit show described itself. Or they are about things that are worse than nothing—sexual exploitation, rebellion, and anger. We need to face the fact that the world has changed drastically in a relatively short period of time and that our children are in peril unless we take wise and loving measures to raise them well in the midst of this cultural minefield.

STANDING AND FIGHTING

Perhaps as you read these thoughts, your most basic impulse is to turn away. Many good parents today simply want to hide from the new problems of the new world. Dorothy might well have done that when her house came to rest in Oz—shutting the door and crawling under the bed in her black-and-white bedroom, hoping the changes would just go away.

But for the sake of our children, we cannot afford to call retreat. Whatever nest we succeed in feathering, sooner or later our children will take wing. Sooner or later they will interact with the people, the places, and the ideas that continue to evolve and to impact one another all around us.

Therefore, we need to realize that our best security is to be informed. Even by homeschooling, filtering computer and television selections, and watching our children closely, we cannot shut out this new world. That would be like trying not to breathe or drink water. God has made us, after all, to be the light of this world—the salt of this earth. We are not to hide but to show ourselves; not only to show ourselves but to show ourselves worthy; not only to show ourselves worthy but to be leaders and transformers of the world around us. This means that not only can we raise wise and capable children of integrity, but we can help our friends and neighbors to do the same. We can become beacons of comforting and healing light in dark times for the family.

The apostle Paul, like you and me, lived in a world of cultural upheaval and challenge. He advised, "Don't copy the behavior and customs of this world, but let God transform you into a new person by changing the way you think. Then you will know what God wants you to do, and you will know how good and pleasing and perfect his will really is" (Romans 12:2 NLT).

This book is about changing the way we think about the home, parenting, our children, and the world in which we live. If we fail to change the way we think, the results may be unthinkable for us.

For example, if we insist on hammering away at home-building with the tools of our parents and grandparents, without taking into consideration the changes in the cultural neighborhood, we may even damage our children. We may cause them to develop anti-Christian attitudes and mind-sets, reacting against the very church and beliefs that we know hold the key to their survival.

If we fail to take an intelligent and measured approach to their anger and the underlying causes of it, we may only throw fuel on the fire. We will only send them into the world with anger issues that are unresolved and certain to disrupt all they undertake as adults.

If we fail to help them make their own black-and-white choices in a world of gray tones, we may push them into making the decisions that are precisely the wrong ones. We will send them out as only more refugees of a confused, frustrated world that has no idea how to choose wisely and causes greater and greater pain.

Introduction

The stakes could not be higher; the issue could not be closer to our hearts; the subjects in the following pages could not be more urgent. Jesus says, "I am sending you out like sheep among wolves. Therefore be as shrewd as snakes and as innocent as doves" (Matthew 10:16). Jesus may well have made such a statement here at the beginning of the third millennium.

SHEEP AMONG WOLVES

Never have the sheep seemed so innocent and the wolves so ravenous. This is a challenging and treacherous new world in which we find ourselves—but it is one filled with promise. We need to recognize that, don't we? The greater the risks, the greater the rewards. If we can somehow help our children to survive and flourish in such a world, what an adventure they will have before them. If they can navigate the rapids of the new cultural diversity, what a joy they will have in interacting with so many fascinating new friends and outlooks. And if they can learn to manage their own anger and impulses, how useful they will be to God. How greatly his hand will be upon their lives, using them as a blessing to their generation and those that follow.

After all, our God has surely not deserted us. No problem, no crisis can overrun his power and sovereignty. Tough times are special times—days filled not only with danger but with promise. Therefore, "be strong and courageous! Do not be afraid or discouraged. For the Lord your God is with you wherever you go" (Joshua 1:9 NLT). Our Lord never promises that anything will be easy. He promises only his presence and power, and that is always enough.

Similarly, the issues and strategies in this book may not be easy, but I believe every parent can master them. I urge you to read the entire book carefully and reflectively, reviewing and restudying the chapters most relevant to your situation. One of the great and comforting secrets of parenting is that the most powerful strategy is a simple one: *Love your child; show your love wisely.* And loving a child wisely, you will discover, is the most natural endeavor we can imagine.

More good news: It all gets easier the longer you persevere. The more you apply your wisdom to the wonderful task of parenting, the easier the whole enterprise becomes. Eventually the right way becomes second nature to you because the true principles *are* natural. God created them and designed us to carry them out. Many of us have been taught wrongly by our own parents and our world, so we have to relearn what is true and right. But as we do so, we find that good and wise parenting slips right into the grooves. We know that things are just as they should be.

As a matter of fact, I would predict that you are already doing many of the right things. The very fact that you picked up this book demonstrates your desire to be a wise parent, and it takes a basic wisdom to desire wisdom. That's why I'm certain you're already a pretty good parent.

Let's learn to be better parents. Let's "change the way we think" on some basic issues, fine-tune the issues on which we're already on the right page, and dedicate ourselves to being the wisest and most loving parents we can be. Then we will raise children who are "strong in character and ready for anything" (James 1:4 NLT)—no matter what lies beyond the blindingly colorful threshold of the world outside our door.

1 THE PARENTING CROSSROAD

It's a defining moment in the life of every potential parent. I'm sure you remember exactly how you felt standing on the threshold of beginning a family of your own.

I'm sure you can recall how every instinct told you that this next step would be the most profound and permanent commitment of your life. You felt the powerful responsibility of taking charge of a young life. Once the door of parenting is opened, there is no turning back.

Facing the question as a young adult, you were a bit eager, a bit awed, a bit afraid. Yet your parents, your siblings, and your friends urged you on impatiently. Sure, marriage was a wonderful thing, they agreed—but parenting was the ultimate! It was the very reason you were placed here on earth. "Just wait," they whispered. "It will change your life *forever*!" You heard those words time and again, and you knew they were true: You could see the joy in the eyes of your friends as they bounced their own infants on their laps. You could observe the obsession as they pulled out their stacks and stacks of photographs and hours and hours of home movies.

In fact, their new-baby tunnel vision was a bit tiring. These ambassadors of parenthood could not or would not discuss *any other subject*. They were totally absorbed in this new world of The Baby. You felt a bit uncomfortable and, yes, a little lonely as you watched them happily vanish into the cocoons they were knitting around themselves and their new families. It was the end of reckless youth and spontaneity.

But you wanted to be like them. You wanted to share the adventure. And when your first child arrived, you understood the joy fully. There in your arms lay a tiny human being—a mysterious and wonderful blend of you, your spouse, and his or her own unique personhood, beautifully crafted by the loving fingers of God. Your child was pink and helpless and could do little more than eat, cry, and soil diapers—yet her very presence seemed to sing out the words of the psalm:

> You created my inmost being;
>> you knit me together in my mother's womb.
> I praise you because I am fearfully and wonderfully made;
>> your works are wonderful,
>> I know that full well. (Psalm 139:13–14)

And so began your grand rite of passage, your initiation into the mystery of human development—the culmination of your very life. There followed all the milestones of baby's early growth and maturity: sitting up, pulling up, walking, the first words, and eventually the epic battles of potty training.

But as your children grew and changed, you learned something crucial: The task of raising children doesn't become easier but grows increasingly complex as the children themselves become older and more complex. And you learned that being a mom or a dad would require all the energy and wisdom you had, and more.

Newborns bring us their own challenges, of course: late-night diaper changes, colic, and the like—but the task is relatively direct, focused, and straightforward compared to that of navigating the volatile waters of a thirteen-year-old daughter at the outset of puberty. And from the uneasy moment when you leave your child in the kindergarten classroom, you realize you can no longer monitor all the variables in that little one's life; there are teachers, classmates, and other outside forces that come into play.

I think you'll agree that the pathway of parenting, from birth to adolescence, is like a trail that begins in a sun-bathed clearing and twists into an ever more tangled forest, with many unanticipated crossroads where difficult decisions must be made. No child is the same; no choice is the same. You think back to those first days with your new baby and realize you had no idea how difficult and demanding this home-building mission would be. Sometimes God is gracious in the naiveté he allows us.

Still, I know you have experienced those inevitable moments of frustration as a parent. We need a plan; we need some understanding. There is nothing in life we desire more than for our children to grow up wise, healthy, and spiritually strong, and so we agonize over the decisions we face at those confusing forks along the path.

Let's take a closer look at the basic variables of children and parenting.

TWO ROADS DIVERGE

You've surely noticed an odd phenomenon in the way different children develop—you have probably seen it within your own family. How can two children be raised similarly yet take different developmental paths?

Let's begin with Tony. Tony was a joy to guide through childhood. There were times when his parents smiled and thought, "This parenting thing is a piece of cake! We had no idea it could be so easy to raise a well-behaved child. There must be something wrong with Bill and Lola down the street, who have had so much trouble with their little boy."

Tony was pleasant and easy to handle—never a discipline problem, never embarrassing out in public. He responded to each new stage of development like a champion, and what a joy it was to share him with extended family, to enjoy his easy obedience, to see him excel in his first years of school.

Then, somewhere around the middle-school years, something changed. The old Tony seemed to—well, to fade out; and some new, unwelcome Tony took his place. Tony's mom and dad racked their brains to figure out what could have brought about this change. Could it have been the transition between elementary and middle school? No, because the teachers and environment were excellent in both cases. Could it be something physical? No, the doctors couldn't find a thing.

The fact remains that Tony somehow became a discontented, angry, defiant, and disagreeable young man. Not only did his A-average plummet in school, but he didn't seem to care. And he was constantly in rebellion against the parents who had adored him and doted on him. He and his parents hung on to their fracturing relationship through Tony's high-school days. He even managed to get into college, but he didn't make it through the first year. By that time he was deeply into drug abuse and got into all kinds of trouble in his dormitory. He left school, got a few dollars from Dad, drove out of town—and no one is certain where he is now.

Then there was the "other" child, Tony's brother, Rick. Rick was a more free-spirited child than Tony: more active, more spontaneous, more prone to laughter and mischief. When he was little, you had to keep an eye on him every minute, but he wasn't a bad child—just an active and curious one. Aunts and uncles said, "Keep an eye on that one! He'll be a handful when he hits the teenage years."

But that's not what happened. Somehow Rick passed right through puberty and adolescence without any of the familiar turbulence. His parents weren't pushed away; they remained his friends and partners in growth and development. He never got into trouble at school, nor did he become rebellious or angry. As a matter of fact, Rick's life and maturity just kept deepening and becoming stronger, right into adulthood.

What made the difference? Is one child just a "bad seed," doomed from the beginning due to some unknown genetic quirk? If children can vary so widely in their behavior, even within a single family, does it even make a difference what strategies for parenting are used?

Of course it does. Although we must recognize the basic mysteries of the human soul—the unknown variables of personal growth and development for a given child—we know that good parenting makes a tremendous difference. Understanding the individual nature of your child—what makes him Rick or Tony or someone else entirely—then parenting proactively, can make all the difference in the world.

We also know that like any other endeavor, good parenting requires a long-term perspective. Let's take a closer look at the importance of that concept.

THE LONG VIEW

It doesn't matter what part of your life we're discussing: You will find the greatest wisdom in considering it from the long view. We call that *perspective,* and perhaps another word for it is *wisdom.*

Perspective is depth perception. We enjoy a view of the Rocky Mountains or the Grand Canyon because we can see the beauty of distance. But human relationships have perspective, too. There is the gift of looking at a child's traits and behavior patterns and understanding how he or she moves years into the future.

In all we do, perspective brings wisdom. If you are living simply for today, you are far more likely to eat that extra helping of ice cream or put off the pressing chores. But if you are wise—if you take two steps back and look at things from the long view—you will act not based on what feels good today, but on what is beneficial for tomorrow and forever. Solomon tells us about the difference in choosing God's wisdom:

> Then you will understand what is right and just
> and fair—every good path.
> For wisdom will enter your heart,
> and knowledge will be pleasant to your soul.
> Discretion will protect you,
> and understanding will guard you. (Proverbs 2:9–11)

Perspective makes a profound difference. Through many years of counseling families, I have noticed how many mothers and fathers parent only in the present moment, rather than taking that long-term perspective we identify with wisdom. They are so focused on Junior's irritating behavior in the here and now that they completely miss the greater implications. And the result of that misdirected strategy is that their parenting is based on the child's actions rather than on his or her needs. Allow me to explain what I mean by actions (or behavior) versus needs.

Jill is very angry and very whiny. She wants to go on that big overnight sleepover at Amanda's house, but it doesn't fit into your family plans. It happens to be the same night when Jill needs to be visiting her grandmother with the rest of your family. So you give your daughter a firm *no,* and the discussion is all over but the whining.

You are tired, your spouse is tired, and the last thing you want to hear is a marathon round of whining. You're just not in the mood. That's what you're thinking right now.

But what is going on in your daughter's mind? Jill doesn't hear any whining; to her it sounds like *reasoning,* like presenting her case. She is emotionally focused on the issue of the sleepover, which to her is presently the world's most urgent issue.

This doesn't mean you should give in, but it does mean you stand together at one of those lesser parenting crossroads— and a number of lesser ones add up. Jill is going to come out of this episode with either unresolved anger or a positive (if painful) learning experience.

PARENTING IN 3-D

If you are focused on the needs of this moment, you'll simply want to turn the spigot that shuts off the whining. You'll focus on bottling up her unappealing behavior, and doing it quickly.

And the likely course of that action is for this incident to become more fuel for Jill's fire: frustration over this and other episodes when, to *her* mind, no one cared about her desires. Frustration then adds up to anger.

But if you are looking at things in more than one flat dimension—if you are focused on the needs of her growth experience, on the lines of perspective that lead to her future and her maturity—you will hear her more clearly and you will approach the crisis in a very different way.

You will still have to deal with the whining and the impossibility of giving Jill her way, but it will not be simply reacting to her behavior. It will be wise action based on Jill's *needs* and on helping Jill come away with something positive from the experience. Not that this is an easy task (we will look at some ways you can do this later on). The key for right now is the focus on long-term issues rather than on the short-term gratification of cutting out unpleasant behaviors.

Think of it another way. If you deal with your children based completely on their behavior, your children will understand that. They will see you as police officers of the home, concerned only with keeping the peace. They will know their actions determine all that goes on in the home, and they can therefore choose their actions to leverage a certain measure of power. And power is such a huge issue in the home. When your children become angry, they will pay great prices in discipline just to test the limits of that power.

Just like the small child who throws a tantrum simply for the attention it brings, your children will act disruptively right on into adolescence and beyond, using unpleasant behavior to control their environment the only way they can. And of course they will hurt not only you and those around them; they will hurt themselves most of all.

Dealing with your children based on their behavior puts them in control of the home. But dealing with them based on their long-term needs lets the parents set the agenda. It keeps the child's journey toward maturity on course.

Reactive parenting, then, is driven by the child's actions. *Proactive parenting* is driven by the child's needs—and by the constant discovery of new growth opportunities.

OLD WISDOM FOR A NEW WORLD

At this point, please allow me to explain why I've prepared this book for you.

For many years I served as a child psychiatrist, a family counselor, and, of course, a loving father. Early on in my career, I discovered that virtually every family that entered my office needed to begin with the same basic information. For example, I observed that most parents had never clearly considered the basic foundational needs of every child.

Rather than spending valuable time and session fees reviewing these, I put together a little book that covered these fundamentals. At the initial agreement to begin counseling with a new patient or family, I could simply hand them the materials and say, "Read these carefully before we meet again."

My pastor, Ben Haden, had a copy of the little book on "how to really love your child." He showed it to his publishing friends, and it became a book that sold more than one million copies nationally and internationally. That was my first experience as an author, and I relate this only to make the point that my files are filled with letters from parents testifying to the success of these approaches. I've proved them myself, of course, through my own children, who have in turn successfully used them with their children.

How to Really Love Your Child and its successors, then, have represented the sum total of my experience in counseling and child psychiatry. I know that these concepts are true and that these strategies can help you raise wise, emotionally fulfilled children who will become adults of spiritual depth and integrity.

In 1996 I retired from practice and looked forward to many mellow years of enjoying my grandchildren and pursuing travel and hobbies. But in that period of time, I've observed changes in our cultural climate that are even more serious than what came before. I've seen a new generation of young people grow up and become parents themselves, with little or no idea about how to love and train their children. Many of them have been raised in the wrong kind of atmosphere—often based on shortsighted behavior modification principles—with heavy-handed discipline resulting in unresolved anger. That anger, in turn, is harming marriages, careers, and sons and daughters.

At the same time, as we've discussed, I've felt our social world slipping into a new and frightening world that needs a new and fresh word to reassure us that no matter what challenges face us, we and our children can make it through—we can trust God as we always have. We can make use of the best wisdom and understanding. And above all, we can love our children and instill in them the wisdom and fortitude to prevail amid the uncertainties of tomorrow.

That's why you're holding this book. Within the total field of parenting, these pages summarize our best past wisdom for the benefit of our future challenges. Before we begin the main portion of this journey, I would like to review our basic understanding of the needs of every child, as presented in *How to Really Love Your Child.*

NEST BUILDING

Parents often focus on the more visible or immediate needs of their children: clothing for the new school year, vegetables for a nutritious dinner, athletics or Girl Scouts for the growing-up experiences we're eager for them to have.

These are all beneficial things, valid elements of the experience of growing up. But of course there are deeper needs that seem less urgent at any given time. They may be "invisible"—less glaring than braces for the teeth or swimming lessons—but these foundational factors will make the difference in how your children come through their growth journey.

I believe there are four essential need areas that all children share. The key to your effectiveness as a parent lies in understanding and meeting these needs—and not one of these can we afford to overlook.

Because each of these four needs is so important, we will spend a significant amount of time in this book examining them individually. A little acronym to help you remember them is NEST, where each letter stands for one of the needs—though we will examine them in a different chronological order.

NEST:
THE FOUR BASIC NEEDS OF CHILDREN

Let me make one very strong point before I present these four needs. Every one of these four is essential and irreplaceable; none should be overly emphasized at the expense of the others. That would be like emphasizing your body's need for water over its need for food and air. It would be like building a house with nothing but bedrooms—no kitchens or baths.

The reason I stress this point, and stress it up front, is that as I teach a seminar and present these four needs to parents, I observe their reactions. They often quickly dismiss some of these, saying, "Oh, sure, I love my kids—no problem there," or "Protection? My kids have no problems in that area." In particular, the parents get to one specific issue—most often, it is discipline—and they beam straight into that one to the exclusion of other areas. One particular issue may have brought them to the seminar, and that's the only one they are prepared to hear about. I know this because, when I open the floor for questions, it's very clear from what they ask that they missed large segments of what has been taught.

I believe this happens because we live in an age of compartmentalized thinking, in which we find it difficult to consider matters holistically. Have you noticed how people can hear biblical sermons all their lives, yet it doesn't occur to them to apply the more obvious concepts to practical living from Monday through Saturday? Have you seen someone emotionally moved by a sermon about love—only to nearly run over people trying to get to the parking lot exit first?

Again it's an issue of the big picture—perspective. Compartmentalized thinking is the natural enemy of the big picture.

Along these lines, we all know that some parents are "feelers"—that is, they are most effectively tuned in to emotional and nurturing issues; others are "thinkers" who are more conceptual. The "feelers" are most likely to pick up on the issues that go along with their orientation. They are affectionate, sensitive to their children's feelings, and laissez-faire about discipline. They struggle to be firm in the issues of training and discipline. On the other hand, the "thinkers" are most interested in considering the pragmatic disciplinary approaches. They can be very firm, but they may fail to meet their children's emotional needs.

Unfortunately, even many of the experts do exactly the same thing. They make a nice, simple, and marketable package of their self-help philosophies by overemphasizing one aspect of balanced parenting—it all comes down to stern discipline, they tell us; or just be affectionate with your child and you'll have no problems.

None of us can get very far with only one section of a map—we need the whole picture. I hope and believe that the four areas outlined below give a much more comprehensive perspective on holistic, proactive parenting. Therefore, I would advise you to reflect carefully on each one of these four needs, considering how they are covered in the case of the children in your family. Each is equally important, and the ones where you're most likely to fail may surprise you.

Here, then, are the four feathers of our NEST:

Nullifying Anger

We need to manage it, model it, and mold our children in a way that they, too, manage it effectively—or this, more than any other factor, can destroy their lives down the road. We will have a great deal to say about training our children to manage their anger.

Emotional Fulfillment

Our children have basic emotional and nurturant needs. In particular, our children need to feel loved. While we all are quick to acknowledge loving our children, we may not know the best way to express our love to them.

Security and Shelter

Our children need to feel safe and protected, both physically and emotionally. This issue becomes even more critical in this new world environment where even elementary schools become danger zones—and where child abuse remains a legitimate threat.

Training and Discipline

It is here that so many parents unknowingly make terrible mistakes. How can we be proactive and need-based in our disciplinary approaches, rather than simply reacting to negative behavior? The answers may not be easy, but there are indeed good answers.

Let us begin our journey, then, with these four needs. If you can meet them effectively, you will raise a child of integrity, strong in character and emotionally healthy. The first we will consider is the need for emotional nurture.

2 BEGINNING WITH LOVE

IN THE LATE 1800S, Henry Drummond wrote a little classic book called *The Greatest Thing in the World*.[1] He studied the immortal love chapter of Scripture, 1 Corinthians 13, and concluded that to love abundantly is to live abundantly. Love, he declared, is the greatest thing there is, for God himself is Love, and to know him is not only to love him but to love others in a way the world, without God, could never imitate.

In the next century, psychoanalyst Erich Fromm wrote another little book, this one called *The Art of Loving*.[2] Though his foundation was less biblical, he expanded Drummond's argument. He observed that the world had become a place where love was more difficult and more necessary than ever; that love is no simple sentiment but an act of devotion, commitment, and courage; that the decision to love is the decision to give all our being sacrificially in a way that flies in the face of every tendency that engulfs our culture.

Love, the greatest thing in the world, is certainly more than our sappy songs and Hollywood romances would have us believe. We all love our children, but we have to ask ourselves whether we are loving them as completely as we possibly can. And we also have to ask the all-important question of whether the love is coming through. The question seems obvious, but don't shrug it aside. Has your child received the profound message that you love her absolutely, unconditionally, and permanently?

There are stories of isolated Pacific islands where Japanese soldiers failed to hear about their nation's surrender to the Allies in 1945, at the conclusion of World War II. For years some of these soldiers lived in caves, scrambled for survival, and remained alert for enemies who no longer existed. Back home, their government was rebuilding and healing. A new life was available. But the message never came through, and these forgotten soldiers kept fighting a desperate war that was no longer being waged.

In the same way, it is terribly tragic to discover children whose message of love and nurture never comes through. They, too, fight a war that is entirely unnecessary. They fight for a love that was always there but never received. There are many things most of us yearn to give our children and cannot—a bigger house, expensive music lessons, better and longer vacations. But one thing that we *all* should have, one thing that has no financial cost at all, one thing that *we believe we have available in abundance,* is love. I have never met counseling clients who said they had no love to give.

Yet all the same, the love fails to come across. Love-starved children scramble for scraps of caring and affection when their lives should be overflowing with it. The fuel that propels a child through his or her first years of life is love, but many of our children are stalled with empty tanks.

As we look at our NEST initials, this one is nested at the very center: *E* for the emotional needs of love and nurture. Apart from air, food, water, and physical shelter, this is the most basic and essential need of every child. Imagine for a moment the plight of trying to train and discipline a child who feels unloved. There would be little success. Imagine how much harder it is to protect and shelter a child from harmful influences when she doesn't have the nurture she needs. Again, the parents cannot succeed. And finally, consider the task of anger management in a loveless relationship. This would be like bailing water out of the *Titanic* with a teacup, for without love, anger continues to grow and fester.

You can easily see why the emotional needs are nested at the very center. This objective is the very beginning of parenting—the urgent need that must be attended to before any other.

So let's attend to it. Let's discover why so many parents in our generation are disconnecting on the most primal level, failing to dispense the primary fuels of love and nurture.

TWO DIFFERENT LANGUAGES

To understand why we have a practical love deficit when there should be none, we have to clearly understand love as it is perceived on both ends—on the part of the giving parent and the receiving child.

We all know the cliché of the housewife sitting at the breakfast table, asking her husband if he loves her. From behind a newspaper comes a vague grunt. The woman continues to nag him for an acknowledgment of affection until the man puts down the newspaper in exasperation and says, "On the day we married, I declared before a minister and all our guests that I love you. If anything changes, you'll be the first to be notified." And he returns to his newspaper.

We understand that love is more than an established condition—more than a contractual agreement. Sydney J. Harris has said, "Love that is not expressed in loving action does not really exist, just as talent that does not express itself in creative works does not exist; neither of these is a state of mind or feeling, but an activity, or it is a myth."[3]

This is easy enough for us to understand. What we don't often realize is that for children, it is even more dramatically true. Adults are verbally oriented people, while children are behaviorally oriented. Adults deal in symbols, syntax, and theoretical concepts more than we realize. Children experience the world in what they see, what they feel, and what they can touch.

Think about the simple and wonderful statement "I love you." We need to say it regularly to those who need to hear it. But when we use the symbolic terminology of that statement with children, it has far greater significance to the speaker than to the hearer. In our minds, we grasp all the implications. We mean, "I cherish you in a very special way. Among all the activities and relationships of my life, I hold you as precious and valuable to me. You bring me life's greatest joy, and I would sacrifice much to make you happy."

Now, do you believe a child grasps the depth of that implicit declaration? No. That child has not lived your life or your depth of experiences. The child's emotional and cognitive vocabulary is far less varied than yours. It stands to reason that your child does not have your maturity and does not grasp deeply significant concepts on your level. As a matter of fact, when the child hears "I love you," it means you have the same pleasant feelings toward him or her that you do about a great number of things in life. You "love" a good hamburger. You "love" baseball, sewing, and various television shows.

Therefore, the parent says, "I love you," and assumes that a profound emotional transaction has taken place. That assumption is largely mistaken. Later on, during the period of adolescence, the child will begin to catch up with the range and subtleties of our expressions. But we need our children to receive our love long before then.

The solution is obvious. We need to learn how to express our love in a language they can readily understand. And there are three primary reasons we need to be very good at putting our love into truly visible action. The first reason we have already discussed. We must use our behavior to *profess* our love—that is, it is the only way to communicate it clearly.

Second, we must use our behavior to *prove* our love. This is not a matter of children's perception; it is a matter of human perception. In practical living, we know that words are cheap. We tend to believe what we see rather than what we hear. Jesus pointed out that we identify trees by their fruit (Matthew 7:16). We identify feelings by their visible evidence. Children are less naive and gullible than we think; they, too, tend to believe what they see and touch.

Third, we must use our behavior to *promote* our love. The fact is that many of us don't know how to demonstrate our feelings because we ourselves were not trained to do so by our parents. Many parents have lived their lives with empty emotional tanks, and they pass the problem on to future generations. When we model affectionate, demonstrative caring and nurture, we are benefiting not just our children but our grandchildren.

I cannot stress enough the need for us to speak *behaviorally* to our children in the things that really matter. But before we address the specifics of how to do that, let's discuss how to create the right atmosphere for your children to receive love and nurture.

A GRACE-BASED HOME

Environments have purposes, and the proper atmosphere is needed to enhance the pursuit of those purposes. For example, your place of business needs a good professional atmosphere, conducive to the kind of work done there. Much thought goes into the office's layout, interior decoration, background music, and so on. A church sanctuary is carefully designed to promote worship and the praise of God. An athletic team takes measures to create an atmosphere of teamwork and championship. With all his talents, Michael Jordan played on some mediocre Chicago Bulls teams until the club developed the intricate chemistry of teamwork. Then they were unstoppable.

Any important setting needs a certain atmosphere in order to be an effective setting for its purpose—including the home. As the cliché goes, there is a difference between a house and a home, and certain elements are required for the former to become the latter. The most crucial rule of all is that your home needs to have an atmosphere of unconditional love— what we also sometimes call *grace*. We're talking about love that is permanently engraved on the heart rather than contractually dependent on the fulfillment of conditions. This love is given its ultimate description in Paul's thirteenth chapter of

1 Corinthians; it is given its ultimate demonstration in the love and self-sacrifice of Christ.

Paul tells us that this brand of love "always protects, always trusts, always hopes, always perseveres. Love never fails" (1 Corinthians 13:7–8). Insert your name and you have a picture of how your children should see you: *My parents always protect me, always trust me, always hope for my best, always persevere in guiding me. They never let me down.*

When my wife and I were young parents, we strove toward unconditional love as an ideal. But we didn't know how to make it happen. And we had no idea just how essential it was that our children understand they were loved *no matter what.* They were loved when they behaved well and when they didn't. They were loved at their best and at their worst. We *had* the love, of course, but we needed to create the atmosphere—the perception of our children that our love was unconditional. When that atmosphere sets in, all our greatest goals as parents become possible. But when our children somehow come to feel that love is fickle and must be earned, we are defeated before we begin.

Later we'll examine the key topic of discipline, but allow me to apply this truth to that area right now. We've discussed the behavior modification model of discipline: Quickly react to the bad behavior with harsh punishment. Many so-called experts put all their emphasis here, and they can point to some quick results as validation. If you quickly spank your child each time he commits the misdeed of the day, you will seem to be getting somewhere at first. The undesired behavior will halt. But over time, there will be anger and resentment to contend with as they reemerge at some later time and in some irrational way.

This will be the subject of our chapter on teaching your

child to manage anger. For the time being, our point is that discipline-based parenting doesn't help us to create an atmosphere of unconditional love and grace. On the contrary, behavior mod sends a message that love is based on adherence to our commands. It gives children exactly what they supposedly "earn" by their actions, whereas grace loves proactively and is not based on any perceived worthiness. Behavior mod creates an atmosphere of fear rather than love. Right on point, John writes, "There is no fear in love. But perfect love drives out fear, because fear has to do with punishment. The one who fears is not made perfect in love" (1 John 4:18).

Reactive parenting is bound to fail because it responds to imperfect children with imperfect (childish) behavior. It creates growing frustration and anger in children who experience law rather than love. Proactive parenting, on the other hand, acts rather than reacts. It is fueled by grace, by a love without limits.

We must constantly ask ourselves, in good times and bad, What is the atmosphere in this home? What is the "emotional wallpaper"? Do our children feel a powerful, nonnegotiable love and grace undergirding all the ups and downs of the family roller coaster? Or do they live with an unspoken fear derived from law-based parenting?

A Biblical Model

Please don't hear me as advocating loose, anything-goes discipline—I am not in the least! That is not an atmosphere of love but an atmosphere of ambivalence. But we need to think about what sets the New Testament of our Bible apart from the Old. In the Old Testament, God's people sought for many generations to earn his favor through perfect obedience, offering animal sacrifices for their failures. Because they were prone to failure, there could never be the right relationship between the Lord and his people. The New Testament shows us how Christ gave himself to us in absolutely unconditional love.

As parents we are to follow his model. We are to love our children in that same way, loving them even when they stumble, setting the pace for the wonderful relationship we are intended to have together. And just as each Christian is transformed a bit more each day to resemble their Lord, our children—through this loving atmosphere—will grow each day to be the wise, well-balanced adults we long for them to be.

As I have mentioned, my wife, Pat, and I discovered more and more that we needed to set this kind of tone in our family. But we knew that unconditional love is no simple task. Christ commands us to love our enemies and pray for those who persecute us, knowing that this is the toughest charge he could give us. It's difficult to feel love for those who cause us pain.

But Christ's point is that this very thing, this seemingly dauntless challenge, is what makes love so special, so miraculous. Of any action or attitude of which humanity may be capable, it is this one that is identified most directly with God: "We know and rely on the love God has for us. God is love. Whoever lives in love lives in God, and God in him" (1 John 4:16). Unconditional love is supernatural. It brings us into the presence and power of God, who loves through us. He will enable you to keep loving your children no matter how bumpy the road becomes.

My wife and I, like all parents, struggled to achieve that ideal—and we didn't always succeed. But in striving to love our children perfectly, we found it helpful to regularly remind ourselves of several factors:

1. Our children are, after all, *children.*
2. Therefore, they will tend to be childish.
3. Childishness annoys us, their parents.
4. Our love helps them move beyond childishness to maturity.
5. Legalistic love will create insecurity, low self-esteem, and prolonged immaturity.
6. Therefore, I accept coresponsibility for their behavior and growth.
7. Gracious love is an investment toward gracious, loving children.

We struggled as all parents do. For my sake and the sakes of my sons and daughter, I prayed constantly for the godliest, most unconditional love I could possibly manifest. I reminded myself, along with the list above, that the emotional welfare, happiness, and personal, social, and spiritual success of my children depended on my creating and maintaining the environment we needed in our home. I know you will do the same.

THE EMOTIONAL TANK

For years I have used the word picture of an emotional tank to explain the needs of children. We are dealing with ideas and concepts that are theoretical and conceptual, and these physical analogies help us take better hold of what we're trying to understand.

In the modern world, most of us can grasp the concept of a fuel chamber. At some point you've probably taken a ride in a car that ran out of gas. It's a jarring experience, because the fuel tank is hidden from sight; we don't think about it as we drive. All we know is that we're moving along smoothly at forty miles per hour, then suddenly we're stranded by the side of the road. The gas tank may not be in plain sight, but you can't go very far without it.

In the same way, people have their own tanks, but the fuels that propel them forward in life are love and nurture. Any sensible driver checks the fuel gauge on a daily basis, making sure the needle is closer to *F* for full than *E* for empty. The driver fills the tank at the proper time to keep the car moving forward. In the same way, you should be attentive daily to your child's behavior, which is the best gauge of the level of his or her emotional tank.

Two important things happen as you keep your child's tank full. First, the emotional state of your child is enhanced. The love she receives reflects whether she is happy or sad, angry or peaceful, attentive or withdrawn. Second, her behavior is determined by that level. How will your child behave when discipline is applied? How obedient will she be on a family outing? How will she do socially with other children? A child who is emotionally content will respond far more effectively in each of these situations.

Your child must have a full emotional tank to be at his or her best in any situation. Most parents think no deeper than the level of discipline, which depends so largely on the status of that emotional tank. If you create the dynamic and positive environment of unconditional love, and provide your children with the caring and nurture they need, they will respond far better to discipline and any of the other elements of training and child rearing in your home. This is why we say that this area is the one nested within—at the very heart of—the four basic needs of children. Training in discipline, protection, and anger management largely depends on your child's emotional well-being.

Remember, love must be learned. Your children don't come into the world with the knowledge of how to express or initiate love on their own. They reflect or return love as they receive it. The child who receives no love will not be capable of giving any. The child who receives limited or legalistic love will be able to offer only that lower form. The child who has never experienced grace will have no conception of it. We have used the metaphor of fuel and tanks, but love is also like a seed that multiplies itself. The love you share with your child will bear fruit in his life, blossoming into loving relationships with his own circle of friends and the family he one day begins. But this will happen only if we show the way.

In the same way, we ourselves cannot express God's love unless we receive it from him. "We love because he first loved us" (1 John 4:19). As he meets our needs, we meet the needs of our children: "My God will meet all your needs according to his glorious riches in Christ Jesus" (Philippians 4:19).

He keeps our tanks full by giving us the joy, the satisfaction, and the love that we need for any situation in life. Each day of our home life, we need to think in these terms: Am I meeting my child's needs? What can I conclude from his behavior? Have I expressed through my own behavior how much I love him?

But by now I can almost hear you saying, "I get the point. But please—get specific! Exactly *how* are we supposed to love our children unconditionally? What can we do to create a grace-based home?"

Let's ponder the practical considerations of filling your children's emotional tanks.

Living the Love

Here is a good rule of thumb for all parents: *Instead of looking first to your children's behavior, begin with your own.*

After all, we are the creators and leaders of the home. Everything begins with us, right? We set the tone, create the atmosphere, establish the rules. It is also our behavior that is the starting point for the behavior of our children.

The average mom or dad fails to parent proactively. He or she will wait until there is a problem to get involved. This, of course, is reactive parenting—the policing mentality. Parents are more like gardeners than police officers. The gardener begins things by planting the seeds, then tends the young shoots and brings the plant to a bloom or a harvest.

That's why you don't want to be a reactive parent. Instead, be active in loving through your behavior. As we've seen, children are behavioral first and verbal only later. We, of course, are verbal. We tend to "act" in the family through speech: having family meetings, lecturing, moralizing, reminding them of the rules, and so on. We need to do a better job of speaking the language of behavior.

There are four primary behaviors we can use to offer unconditional love to our children. Let's consider three of them in depth. The fourth, training, will be covered in our discipline chapter.

1. Eye Contact. "Mommy, look at me!" Billy is calling urgently from the top of his swing-set slide. Mommy looks and smiles, and Billy gets ready to perform his special trick.

Just then, having smiled, Mommy turns back to her rosebushes.

Billy sees that and catches the edges of the slide to stop

himself. "Mommy! Look!" Again Mommy looks and offers a slightly less enthusiastic smile.

This time Billy waits to see if Mommy is going to look away. When she does, he calls, "Mommy!"

Mommy sighs heavily. "Okay! Okay! Could you hurry up and do whatever it is you're going to do?"

Billy hesitates, then his lower lip slides out and his expression becomes partly cloudy. Sulking, he crosses his arms across his chest.

"I declare," says Mommy to herself, pruning petals. "It's *impossible* to make him happy."

We've all been there, haven't we? Children want our attention—this we know. But there's something in particular that we often miss. They crave eye contact. It's not enough for you to listen or to be aware of what they're doing. Even if he's simply reading a story he's written or describing an incident from school, your child wants to see your eyes because the eyes tell the story. They tell not only whether we're attentive but also whether we're sympathetic, whether we're angry or bored, and most of all whether we *understand* the precise thing they want us to understand at that point. If there's something special about that trick on the slide, your eyes reveal whether you "get it"—whether you caught the special thing. If there's some particular point to the classroom story, your eyes reveal whether you grasp that point.

Your eyes are the visible evidence of the connection between you. They link you together in a moment of shared understanding, the precious communication we all crave. I find that many parents have never stopped to consider this simple element of love.

Yet we ourselves feel the same way about eye contact, don't we? Remember that conversation recently—at church or at the office—where you were making some important point and your friend kept looking over your shoulder at someone or something else? You were offended, irritated. Remember when you were giving important instructions to your spouse and you insisted on eye contact before speaking? It wasn't even a conscious action, just a natural instinct. We have an immediate distrust and dislike of those who won't look us in the eye. And every good salesperson is trained, before anything else, to make eye contact. It's important to us, so how much more important is it to your children?

It is important enough that when you take care to stop what you're doing and look your children in the eye, they feel the love. And it's important enough that if you don't make eye contact, your children feel as if they're not even there; not even important enough for Mom's or Dad's attention. They feel as if they're no more than objects in the room, like potted plants. We need to look them in the eye, and we need to teach them to do the same.

An infant's eyes will begin to focus at about two to four weeks of age. The most primary image for that infant is a human face, and the most primary part of that face is the eyes. The child begins to develop cognitively and gain coordination, and she searches for another set of eyes—especially her mother's eyes. When she finds them, she "locks on" to them like a radar signal. Already a newborn child is trying to fill her emotional tank, in the most basic, primitive form of communication, because that is all that is available at her level.

We can even see that God designed the child's eyes to make

contact with her mother during breast-feeding. As she feeds physically with her mouth, she feeds emotionally with her eyes.

By the time that child is five, so much of her personhood will be established: her basic personality, modes of thinking, style of speech, and much more. How vitally important that by this time, the child has been filled with the "look of love" from parents, relatives, and friends.

So basic, so simple, and yet few parents ever think about it.

2. Touch. Parents also fail to realize the importance of physical contact. We all know the importance of the good, warm hug. But most moms and dads only touch their children "on business"—that is, when they have some direct purpose. Yes, there is the hasty good-night kiss and hug or the good-bye kiss before school. But for the most part, parents confine physical contact to duties such as bathing or dressing their children, putting them in the car, or other pragmatic occasions.

Think of those times you've received the unexpected hug or the kiss on the cheek from someone important. There is an almost electric surge of love and warmth we receive from the simple touch of another human being, particularly one we care about. And there could be nothing simpler than embracing your child at the odd moment, putting her in your lap, or giving her a big kiss on the cheek "just because." That's powerful fuel for the emotional tank. Yet Americans have one of the lowest rates of casual touch in the world, according to research. French parents touch their children three times more often than parents in America.[4]

Reactive parenting doles out both discipline and affection based on behavior. But when you apply the positive power of physical touch for no "official" reason, your child sees that love is not connected to behavior. You are powerfully validating the presence of unconditional love and grace in your home.

In biblical times, the touch of a parent was enshrined as something holy and empowering. Fathers gave a blessing to their sons. Genesis 27 shows the physical and powerful blessing Isaac gave to Jacob (though, of course, Jacob was deceiving him on this occasion). The embrace of the father, combined with words of benediction, was a kind of human extension of the blessing we receive from God as his children. Fathers in particular need to take note of the positive well-being they can impart to their children through the combination of touch and verbal affirmation.

What are the varieties of physical contact? After all, you can hug or kiss your child only so many times in a day. But many other levels of physical touch can be helpful: touching the shoulder or arm, mussing the hair, scratching the back, poking playfully in the ribs—you can find many varied expressions of affection.

Study after study has verified the importance of physical touch to human well-being. It's not a luxury or an option but something essential and irreplaceable. The University of Miami School of Medicine Touch Research Institute demonstrated that touch actually promotes not only emotional growth but physical growth as well. Prematurely born infants receiving three fifteen-minute periods of slow, firm massage strokes each day experienced a staggering 47 percent greater weight gain than infants not receiving this attention. The massaged children also demonstrated superior sleep, alertness, and physical activity.[5]

Autistic children are known to dislike being touched. But studies have shown that massage therapy helps them, too. A group of autistic children were given a half-hour massage two times a week for five weeks. At the end of the study, the massaged children showed significantly less "off-task" behavior and better social relations with their teachers.[6]

Quite clearly, newborn babies and small children benefit powerfully from simple human touch. But is there any reason to believe that need goes away? Of course not. As a matter of fact, appropriate physical contact is particularly effective during the adolescent years. It's important, of course, that you've carried over this behavior from their early years. During this period, many teenagers grow silent or sullen. It becomes more difficult for us, the verbally oriented adults, to converse with them. It may be very difficult to maintain eye contact, and even focused attention (our third strategy) may be rebuffed.

Should you worry about your teenager's emotional tank when he doesn't seem to want to be around you at all? Yes, you should—more than ever. An adolescent has a number of challenges and struggles and new issues on his mind, so don't misread his behavior and withdraw when he needs love the most. It is in these situations that a good hug and regular physical contact will come to the aid of your relationship. Pick your occasions carefully—Ecclesiastes 3:5 tells us there is "a time to embrace and a time to refrain" from embracing—but make sure you touch and hug at the right unexpected moment. Parents who do so make it through the teen years with far less stormy weather. As a matter of fact, teenagers with full emotional tanks will be less likely to manifest some of the other unpleasant behaviors.

Now combine the two opportunities we've discussed: eye contact and touch. What would you expect to be the result of offering both at the same time? When you look your child in the eye and touch him warmly—casually, frequently, appropriately—you are injecting something powerful, priceless, and precious into his emotional growth and development. Your child feels truly loved, simply for who he is and not what he does or doesn't do. You are setting the tone for a home of authentic, supportive love. Then, when the occasion for discipline arises, you have laid down the foundation for the lesson to be taught more effectively.

Think about the physical touch in your family—spouse to spouse, parent to child, child to parent. There is simply no substitute for it. Take full advantage of one of the most powerful caring and nurturing strategies in the human emotional arsenal.

3. Focused Attention. It is so wonderfully simple to look our children in the eye and apply the power of human touch. But our third strategy, focused attention, takes a greater sacrifice. This is a generation in a hurry—the age of the tight appointment calendar. Even our children are stressed out from too many activities. And here's another demand for our time: focusing on our children.

Yes, we've heard it all before, and it's nothing new. It was a century or so ago that Mark Twain said, "We are always too busy for our children; we never give them the time or interest they deserve. We lavish gifts upon them; but the most precious gift, our personal association, which means so much to them, we give grudgingly."

We need to ask what could be more important. We have all heard the truism that no dying business executive ever expressed the observation that he wished he had spent more time at the office. But every parent experiences that flat feeling of the empty nest—that longing to have our children young and carefree again, running around the house, playing baseball, or going to Girl Scouts. If we could invent a time machine in those moments of felt loss, we would gladly attend a few more ball games with that son or take a leisurely stroll at the mall with that daughter.

Marcelene Cox has said that "parents are often so busy with the physical rearing of children that they miss the glory of parenthood, just as the grandeur of the trees is lost when raking leaves."[7] We're focused on the details, raising as well as raking, until the autumn of our lives when the nest is bare and the leaves have fallen. We need to have made not only memories but powerful emotional connections.

Your appointment calendar is a map of your heart; like your checkbook, it shows what matters most in your life. When your children don't have enough of what we've come to call "face time" with you, once again their emotional tanks are running on empty. Daddy-and-daughter dates or a few minutes in the yard throwing the football are powerful acknowledgments of love. And the more our children see us sacrificing our time and energy and television shows and naps to do these little things, the more they know they are loved.

The question I most often receive about focused attention is this: "Won't I spoil my child by following him around to all his activities?" No, not at all. Spoiling is a training issue, not an attention issue. Train your child properly, using appropriate discipline, and your child will not be spoiled. Children who are unloved present a much greater problem today than children who are spoiled.

If you feel too busy, too driven, think of the priorities of Jesus. He had three years to change the world, three years for the work and ministry that would be the most important in human history. Yet observe his regard for both touching and focusing attention on children in this passage from Scripture:

> People were bringing little children to Jesus to have him touch them, but the disciples rebuked them. When Jesus saw this, he was indignant. He said to them, "Let the little children come to me, and do not hinder them, for the kingdom of God belongs to such as these. I tell you the truth, anyone who will not receive the kingdom of God like a little child will never enter it." And he took the children in his arms, put his hands on them and blessed them. (Mark 10:13–16)

The parents above were eager for the hand of Jesus on their children, and we share their desire. But before our children can ever be touched by the Lord, they must be touched and loved by their parents. We need to find every opportunity to lavish on them the love and attention they need. The psalmist reminded us that our children are "a heritage from the LORD, children a reward from him" (Psalm 127:3). Nothing in our lives, apart from loving our precious husbands or wives, could be as important.

By the way, lavishing love on your children is not the same as lavishing *gifts* on them. That's a natural instinct for many parents, but it's not a good way to fill emotional tanks. Any child is thrilled to receive a toy or other material gift. However, her genuine emotional needs require emotional solutions. The only gift you can give your child that makes a difference is yourself, and this gift is measured not in dollars and cents but in hours and minutes. Love them now, and not only do you have the joy and fulfillment that brings for parent and child alike, you have the prevention of problems and heartache down the road—problems much less likely at the hands of children with full emotional tanks.

TYRANNY OF THE URGENT

Charles E. Hummel wrote a wonderful little book called *Freedom from Tyranny of the Urgent.*[8] His simple point was that we spend most of our lives allowing the important things to be overlooked in favor of the urgent things. Life's truly important matters don't tend to loom before us ominously. We fill up the gas tank right on schedule, because that is *urgent*—we've got to get to the office. There's no daily imperative to make us fill up our children's emotional tanks, even though it's *much* more important. So many truly significant tasks go uncompleted because we buckle under to the tyranny of the urgent.

Think about your life. If it's anything like mine, it's a colossal collection of little yet urgent things that have to be done: brushing our teeth, cleaning the snow off the walk, working on the tax return, buying a birthday gift. All of these represent valid uses of our time. But what about those things for which life doesn't provide built-in reminders?

It could be that you and I will stand in heaven someday, looking down on the earth and the legacies we have left. There will be mountains of eternally insignificant accomplishments; and there will be hurting people saying, "I was hungry, and did you feed me?" There will be lonely friends we might have comforted. There will be personal talents we never developed, with which we might have done powerful things for God. We may stand as Ebenezer Scrooge did when he was the guest of the Ghost of Christmas Past—looking back on what really mattered but was missed.

You may be thinking, How gloomy! But perhaps this is your wake-up call. We each start the day with the same resource in our hands: twenty-four precious hours. Wonderful good can be done in a single allotment of that resource. Always remember that whatever your calendar reads, this is the day the Lord has made; and the Lord longs to put his imprint on it for you and those you love. This day offers unique opportunities to connect with your children, to fill their emotional tanks, to enhance the atmosphere of unconditional love and grace.

Paul has our final thought for this chapter. He wrote, "Be very careful, then, how you live—not as unwise but as wise, making the most of every opportunity, because the days are evil" (Ephesians 5:15–16). Evil indeed, then as now. Your child is vulnerable to all the fears and dangers of this new world. But if you love your child and transmit that love, he or she will be fully equal to any challenge life can provide.

BILLY IS BACK AT THE TOP OF THE SLIDE.

"Mommy, look at me!" he calls.

Mommy turns around and smiles. "What's up, Billy?"

"I've got a new trick!"

Mommy drops the pruning shears and walks over to the slide. "Not another one!" She laughs. "You must be the world's greatest sliding genius!" Her face is close to his as she says it. She looks her son in the eye as she smiles and ruffles his hair. "Now let's see that trick."

Billy does his thing, whooshing down the board with a loud battle cry. At the bottom, Mommy scoops him into the air as Billy shrieks with laughter. Both of them land in a hilarious heap on the ground. Then they knock off the dust, walk over to the swings, and take their seats. Higher and higher they swing, side by side—laughing, enjoying the day, and getting a little bit closer to heaven with each new push.

3 BASIC TRAINING: THE DISCIPLINE PUZZLE

IMAGINE YOURSELF IN AN OFFICE environment. It's late in the afternoon of "one of those days."

Today, you've just about had your fill of the customer-service department. The phone has been ringing off the hook. It's as if the starting lineup of the All-Obnoxious Team of the business world has targeted you today. You haven't even had a second to deal with any of the other issues in the back of your mind (family issues, a misunderstanding with a friend, a problem at church). *Enough is enough.*

Thankfully, the phone calls finally slow down. You take a deep breath, come out from behind your desk, and plop your tense and tired frame into a chair facing your supervisor's desk. Your supervisor looks up impatiently from a file as you place your hands on the sides of your head in mock panic. *"Aaaaaaaaaaargh!"* you rattle in demonstration of your emotional state.

Your supervisor inspects you coolly, then returns to his file.

"Ugh!" you continue. "I can't *stand* days like this!"

"Cut it out," says your supervisor.

"Huh?" you ask, a bit surprised.

"Your behavior is unattractive."

"Well, it's just that I needed to let off a little steam. It's been . . ."

"I don't care what it's been. Either behave professionally or stay in your cubicle."

"But . . ."

"Conversation is over, understood? Now go back to your desk and think about your behavior."

WOULD YOU ENJOY WORKING FOR THAT KIND OF BOSS? Perhaps you already have. It's easy for us to see exactly what's wrong with the supervisor's approach: a complete lack of human feeling—of *empathy,* to be precise. Empathy is the ability to understand someone else's feelings; not only to understand but to "walk a mile in their shoes," as the old saying goes.

Selfish people (with which this world is well stocked) are imprisoned within their own limited perspectives. As a leader, this person will tend to be strict and autocratic. When given a choice, we'll choose the empathetic leader over the tyrant every time. We naturally admire and follow that type.

In the situation we've just seen, the supervisor's approach was: How can I put a stop to this unpleasant behavior? A more perceptive and helpful question would have been: What does my coworker need? Notice that either approach would ulti-mately address the rattled behavior of the stressed-out service rep. But the autocrat applies force (creating frustration and resentment), while the caring leader reaches out and co-operates for a solution (creating fellowship and loyalty).

It stands to reason, doesn't it? It has been said that the greater our power, the gentler should be our downward reach. It's not simply a matter of wanting to follow a servant-leader who helps us manage our burdens; we know that we will *be more successful* under that kind of leader.

If you take hold of that truth and apply it to parenthood, you will see it's a perfect—and surprisingly enlightening—fit. When a child behaves in an unpleasant way, most parents react in the manner of the supervisor we've just observed. They focus on the outward behavior and use their authority to stop it immediately. Again, the better approach is to focus on the need rather than the symptom. Like a good leader in any other setting, the parent listens, draws a conclusion about the real problem, and works *with the child* to make whatever change is necessary.

FAMILY DISCIPLINE AND SELF-DISCIPLINE

Need-based parenting is not a weak, hands-off approach; it is precisely the opposite. Some parents see this type of restraint as "too much love," prone to spoil the child (especially after hearing their own parents quote the misused proverb "Spare the rod and spoil the child" countless times). These parents withhold love and impose punishment, thinking this will strengthen the child. This just leads to the "punishment trap," causing the entire parent-child relationship to revolve around behavior rather than love. There is ultimately nothing "strong" or leaderlike about imposing authority on a child. Rather, it takes a great deal more self-discipline and momentary wisdom to recognize the child's need and help him or her meet it.

Just as you'll be more successful under a feeling, caring, and burden-sharing boss, your child will flourish and develop far more positively with empathetic leaders as parents. Let me underscore again that this will happen because you have set a tone of unconditional love and grace in your home. Your child will understand that behavior and misbehavior—though important—are not the central issue. The child's need comes first. And the older the child grows, the more she will understand and appreciate that love.

Let's also face the unpleasant truth that the primary reason a parent focuses on behavior is the selfish reason. Moms and dads rarely stop to think about it that way, but it's true. They simply don't want to be around unpleasant behavior—after all, who does?

None of us enjoy complaining, crying, whining, or any other childish maneuvers. The first impulse we have is to address the behavior, as we'd address squealing brakes on a car. We don't need one more aggravation in these tiring times. It's a new world with new stresses and pressures: more homes where both parents work, more activities and demands on time, more poor influences for our children. Even in our churches, it's a new world where congregations reflect the same stress load as the rest of the world.

Amid all the turmoil adults face, it's all the more unsettling to hear the "squealing brakes" of childishness. It's all the more tempting to simply say, "Cut it out!" and dig in our heels.

But our children are fragile, flesh-and-blood creatures in the tangled process of human development; their destinies are on the line. We need to handle them a bit more carefully than we handle the iron and chrome of our automobiles. Machines are destined for the junk heap, but children are eternal creatures from the hand of God. While Paul wrote the following advice for adults within the family of God, it applies also to the family at home:

> Do not use your freedom to indulge the sinful nature; rather, serve one another in love. The entire law is summed up in a single command: "Love your neighbor as yourself." If you keep on biting and devouring each other, watch out or you will be destroyed by each other. (Galatians 5:13–15)

I have seen parents all but destroyed by the heartbreak of grown children who ultimately made the wrong choices. Believe it or not, there are parents who are now coming to me in tears. "I haven't seen my daughter in five years," they might say. "She seems to want nothing to do with me, and I can't figure out why." The *why* seems to be that grown children from Christian homes are carrying furnaces of resentment within them—and their parents never even suspected. We must take great care in how we deal with our children. *Before we can achieve family discipline, we must achieve self-discipline.*

WHO'S IN CONTROL HERE?

Let's visit two households that are coping with the discipline issue—and that central issue of who is in control.

We visit Household A just in time for a big football game on television. Mom and Dad have invited their friends the Miltons from across the street. The popcorn is popped, soft drinks are in the refrigerator, and everyone's sharing friendly chat until game time.

Then Sharon, four years old, suddenly descends upon the scene. Here we go again . . .

Sharon is making enough noise to drown out the adult chat. First, she wants her own bowl of popcorn. Then she wants to know why everyone can't watch her cartoon tape instead of the football game. Then she wants to show off a new toy.

Mom and Dad, of course, valiantly try to get Sharon under control. But the little girl quickly erupts into a screaming tantrum. The Miltons, who have no children, are fidgeting awkwardly. Why should the occasion be disrupted for them? So Mom and Dad cave in, meeting pretty much all of Sharon's demands.

"I can't figure it out," Mom says later as she cleans up the bowls and glasses. "Sharon always seems to go into these tirades at the worst possible times—when we're around other people."

The following week, the Miltons visit another home in the neighborhood. Things are considerably quieter in Household B. As soon as the Miltons come in, Dad immediately turns to his small son and snaps, "Stop playing with those blocks and pick up this room! Don't you see we have guests?" Eddie, the son, is at the very beginning of whining—but Dad claps his hands. "I mean, *now*!" he barks. "Or you're going to be in *deep trouble*!"

The Miltons feel just as awkward as they did in Household A. This home has the atmosphere of a work camp. A sullen teenager skulks through the room at one point, he and Dad glare at each other, and nothing is said. The teenager slams the door as he goes out. The Miltons have heard troubling stories about the teenage boy.

The Miltons are puzzled. They've always looked forward to starting a family. They wonder whether their family will be more like

- Household A: Kids in control—chaos
- Household B: Parents in control—cold war

Or possibly:

- Household C: Neither of the above

We would all like to hope for a third option, wouldn't we? But in recent years, I have seen a polarizing effect, with homes gravitating more to either the undisciplined, chaotic model (A) or the reactive, behavior-based model (B).

I believe things have grown worse because of the new world effect. Parents are spread thin. More and more of them are single parents, for example, and they're courageously trying to hold everything together by the exertion of superhuman effort. And two-parent homes may not always be that much better, as we see more marriage tensions and conflicts than ever. Finances are spread thin. And because of mobility and career, fewer extended families—grandparents, aunts, and uncles— are around to lend support.

Tension is high, parents are tired, and the child senses all this and feels insecure. Misbehavior is often a cry for attention and reassurance. But it also may be the straw that breaks the camel's back for a stressed-out mom or dad. A parent may capitulate rather than risk a noisy tantrum situation. This problem, incidentally, will only grow worse in time if the parents don't take control of the household. Or the parent will take the reactive, punishment-driven approach and come down on misbehavior like a hammer on a gnat.

The third option is the one we advocate in this book and particularly in this chapter. Let's establish that no parent should ever lose control of the household. If you realize that your child knows how to successfully push your buttons, you have a situation that is bad for everyone, particularly the child.

On the other hand, *firm* need not imply *inflexible*. A firm approach is successful when the child knows he is loved and when his emotional tank is full. A parent must hit that right balance between firm and fair, strict and loving. He or she must retain composure at all times.

It's crucial that we understand what discipline is—and is *not*.

THE TRUTH ABOUT DISCIPLINE

If I were to play the word-association game with you and give you the word *discipline,* what response would most quickly come to your mind? Your most immediate reply might suggest your perspective on this complex and misunderstood concept.

Did you think of the word *punishment*? Many people confuse discipline and punishment, and that's precisely why we need to define these terms carefully.

Punishment is not the same as discipline but one variety of it—the most negative kind. Punishment should not even be considered the most important part of discipline. It is the final option, though it's an option you will certainly have to use occasionally. But before any negative form of training or discipline is employed, we should exhaust all our options from the positive side.

We all would prefer to get each of life's cooperative tasks done in a pleasant setting. At work, as we've discussed, we would surely rather be supervised in a spirit of teamwork rather than tyranny. The task of raising children is much the same. One of the primary reasons so many parents are struggling to raise their children is that they've allowed their relationships with their children to deteriorate to a spirit of conflict. They find themselves practicing *reactive* parenting—waiting and expecting the child to misbehave, then reacting with the corresponding sanction. No wonder so many of our children are emerging into society with an anger-based approach to living, for the home becomes (to our children) a microcosm of the world that awaits them. If home is a matter of two entrenched armies, then the world must be one more hostile enemy awaiting them.

This is why I emphasize that we should exhaust every *positive* option for training and discipline before resorting to punishment. *The most important part of discipline is for parents to make a child feel loved.* Fulfill that mandate, then proceed to the next most important: *Train your children in mind and character to enable them to become self-controlled and constructive members of society.* Discipline is all about training, and it takes advantage of every available form of communication:

- Personal example

- Verbal instruction

- Written requests

- Teaching

- Play experiences

Every one of those opportunities is a positive one. Each one approaches your child respectfully as a thinking, feeling human being capable of positive growth. None of them reduce your child to a stimulus-response mechanism capable of learning only by negative behavior-mod techniques.

Simply *love* and *train,* in that order, and there is no reason you can't raise your child to be a wise and well-balanced adult, strong in character and self-concept. The child with the full emotional tank identifies with the parents who provide the love; she is ready to learn, to be positively molded. The child who does not identify with the parents, but resents their negative orientation, will be ready only to rebel.

The most important issue of discipline, then, is once again the issue of love—the theme of your household, if you are wise. We need to understand not only our own capacity to love but the child's own capacity in this regard. How does your child express love?

THE LOVING CHILD

You feel and express love in a way that is determined from the sum of your life experiences: how you have been loved, how you have craved love, how you've been taught, and the ups and downs of your "love life."

It stands to reason that your child doesn't share your accumulated life experience. Any child is immature physically, emotionally, intellectually, and spiritually, and therefore loves immaturely as well.

Imagine the typical parents, Craig and Amanda. When they met, they had a mutual attraction that grew into love. In the beginning, it was a kind of "transaction," in that they gave each other little gifts and performed the courting ritual that is ingrained in their culture. We would call this a *reciprocal* love, in that it was based on give-and-take (though it seemed much more romantic than that). As they moved into the commitment of marriage, the transactional relationship continued: He loved her by using his Christmas bonus to buy her a nice ring; she loved him by fixing him his favorite meal or maintaining an orderly household.

Craig and Amanda, like most of us, aspire to the higher form of love, the *unconditional* type that Paul described in 1 Corinthians 13. At that level, I love you—period; no transaction applies. As their love deepened over the years, there was more unconditional love and somewhat less of the "transactional." Craig and Amanda developed at least an instinctive understanding of these forms of love.

But their child, Kimberly, was capable of neither one. A child doesn't even understand the give-and-take element of relationships. Her love is primarily a matter of the felt need, of an instinctive craving, as she knows she needs to feel affection. Her tank needs to be filled. Parents, too, have emotional tanks; theirs need to be filled not only by their spouse and friends but certainly by the beloved child. That's the last thing on Kimberly's mind. She simply hasn't attained that level of emotional maturity. On top of that, she is verbally immature and behavior-based.

Therefore, love for Kimberly works like this: When her emotional tank is filled—when Mommy and Daddy pay enough attention to her, play with her enough, give her plenty of eye contact, physical contact, and focused time—then she will be content, and her behavior will reflect that contentment. When her emotional tank is not full, she instinctively needs to ask, Do you love me? The question, however, will not be asked in words; it will be acted out.

Sometimes Mommy and Daddy have other things on their minds. That's life. There comes a time when there are significant issues with Daddy's job, and his state of mind affects that of his wife (remember, her emotional tank needs regular filling, too). In this less than perfect setting, Kimberly isn't getting the attention she requires. Behaving *well* doesn't seem to help—she tried to sit in her daddy's lap, and Daddy gently pushed her away. Mommy said, "Can you go play with your dolls, Kimmy? Mommy and Daddy need to talk right now." Misbehavior is the one sure way to get attention, to find out if Mommy and Daddy still care about her.

PAUL AND PARENTING

If they are reactive parents, Craig and Amanda fail to see the misbehavior as a love-cry. They are angry because she is picking the worst time of all to "act up." Again, they're failing to take into account her emotional maturity (or lack of it). She doesn't know it's the worst time of all. She only carries an all-important need for a full emotional tank. *And the emptiness of that tank is the most common cause of misbehavior.*

Is all misbehavior due to the felt need for love? No, there are other causes. But this is the cause we should look to first.

For Craig and Amanda, it stands to reason that Kimberly should earn her love and affection by "being a good girl," that is, behaving in a mature manner. It's an impossible demand. Behavior to the child is the testing ground for love, and there is always going to be a certain amount of misbehavior. Unless these parents understand the setting from their child's point of view, they will be frustrated, reactive, and prone to plant seeds of frustration and bitterness in their child.

Paul wrote, "Fathers, do not exasperate your children; instead, bring them up in the training and instruction of the Lord" (Ephesians 6:4). To another church he wrote, "Fathers, do not embitter your children, or they will become discouraged" (Colossians 3:21). He is referring in this passage to both parents, though he speaks to fathers here. Readers in his time would have understood that mother and father alike should heed his advice. And it's worth noting that the Roman culture of New Testament times was very harsh in the area of discipline: Child beatings were the common form of "training."

Paul's words of loving nurture and training were radical and striking in a way hard for us to imagine. His concept of parenthood implied an uncommon respect for the personhood and dignity of children. This brand of love is at the heart of our faith. It reflects the love of God, who, through his Son, meets us where we are, regardless of our own emotional and spiritual immaturity. He loves us with compassion and empathy so that we identify with him as he has identified with us. "We love because he first loved us" (1 John 4:19). Our children, too, will love as we first love them.

Our Christian faith moves us every day toward godliness—not by the fuel of fear and punishment but by the fuel of grace and limitless love. This is the difference between Old Testament and New Testament faith. We should mirror that gracious love of God in our love for our children—meeting them where they are, loving them unconditionally, and recognizing the need rather than reacting to the behavior—until they identify with us, want to be like us, and cooperate with us in their mental, emotional, and spiritual growth.

IDENTIFYING THE NEED

So we find Amanda and Craig deep in discussion about Craig's job situation. This is a tremendous issue that will affect the whole family. But Kimberly has no understanding of that fact. The only reality for her is the sudden absence of all the signals that say *love* to her: eye contact, physical affection, and focused attention. Do her parents still love her? They know they do, we know they do, but Kimberly is running on empty. She needs the fuel that maintains a smooth emotional system.

Kimberly throws a toy across the room—something she's been told not to do. It's a part of her dollhouse, and it thumps against the wall. Craig is immediately perturbed; his nerves are on edge anyway. He raises his voice as he tells his daughter to stop.

But perhaps Amanda looks beyond the behavior. Kimberly is a well-loved child who isn't particularly prone to misbehavior. She seems to have thrown the dollhouse section for no good reason. So Amanda thinks, What's up with Kimberly? Why has she done something she knows will get her into trouble?

Here is the first question a wise parent will ask: *Does my child need her emotional tank filled?*

"Wait a minute," she whispers to Craig. "Let's not punish her quite yet. You and I have not paid much attention to her because of this job crisis. Maybe she just needs a little love."

Craig shrugs, and Amanda stops to attend to her daughter. She discovers that Kimberly had several things to say in the last half-hour, and no one would listen. The problem is easily solved, and Mommy and Daddy can finish their conversation without any trouble from Kimberly, who is now humming as she colors a picture.

I remember a time I had an experience close to this one, when my sons were nine and five. As they met me at the airport after a conference I attended, I was eager to describe my experiences to my wife. On the way home, Dale, my younger one, kept saying, "Dad?" I mainly ignored him as I continued talking to Pat.

By the time we had come to our front door, Dale had lost

his patience. He was whining and crying at every little excuse. He was picking at his older brother so that even David had become upset.

I was tired and frustrated by the disruption. I wanted to fix the behavior, and my first instinctive thought was the wrong one: How can I make him stop?

Pat, with a wisdom that exceeded mine, suggested that I practice what I preach. So I changed my question to, What does Dale need? It stood to reason that a five-year-old boy had missed his father for the last several days. He wanted strong reassurance that his father, who had deserted him for a time, still loved him. As he continued to call my name and I continued to ignore him, he certainly didn't receive the affirmation he needed. By whining, crying, and being disruptive, he was asking, "Do you still love me after being gone so long and then acting as if that didn't affect my life?"

If I hadn't stopped to think about this and my behavior had grown worse (stern voice, stricter punishment), then his behavior would have grown worse, too. His insecurity and need to be loved would have grown more urgent. But realizing what I did, my whole outlook changed. I took Dale off to the side and held him quietly. Words weren't even necessary—an action is worth a thousand of them, and ten thousand to a child. He sat quietly and soaked up the affection and nurture he craved. As his emotional tank filled, he began to talk happily. Soon he was in the next room, contentedly playing with his brother. Peace was restored.

Is it always so simple? We wish it were so. Sometimes misbehavior has other root causes. If you are certain the emotional tank is not empty, your next question should be, *Is this a physical problem?* That's the second leading cause of misbehavior. Your follow-up questions are, *Is my child in pain? Is he ill? Is she tired, hungry, thirsty?* If you discover the cause to be physical, the cure is generally quick and simple.

FIVE WAYS TO CONTROL BEHAVIOR

Love does not conquer all, though it goes the greater part of the journey. There are times when some other issue is behind the misbehavior. There are times when you'll have to go the length of punishment. You should never lose control of your household. When a child attempts to take control through disruptive behavior, you can respond in five different ways. Two of these are positive, and they're the preferred approaches. Two are negative, though you will need them on occasion; and one is neutral and should be used with special care. Here are the five and their positive-negative orientation:

Requests	Positive
Commands	Negative
Gentle physical manipulation	Positive
Punishment	Negative
Behavior modification	Neutral

Requests and Commands

It's far more pleasant to be asked than to be ordered. When you make a request of a child, you tend to ask in a more musical, soothing voice. Requests take the form of a question, with inflection rising at the end: "Would you put away your *blocks?*" This helps control a child's behavior. As a matter of fact, it is more influential for anyone's behavior.

There are other positive points about requests. They embody respect for the one on the receiving end. Even more, we are sending the message that we expect a child to take responsibility for his or her own behavior. Requests offer the status of free will. There is an implied cooperation between the questioner and the correspondent. But is authority being surrendered? Not at all. On the contrary, we respect those who respect us. We naturally feel they're acting out of the desire for what is best for us.

Inevitably, of course, the request will fail. Children are immature, and at times they will test the limits. In these situations—only if and when requests fail—the parent needs to use *commands.*

Commands are obviously more negative in nature. Most people tend to resent being ordered to do things. Where questions have a musical inflection, commands are issued in lower, naturally threatening tones. They offer no respect, no cooperation, no option. And most important, they shift all power and therefore responsibility to the one who commands. Growth and maturing are no longer matters of cooperation but matters of coercion by the one in power. One of the many reasons this doesn't work is that it makes growth less desirable as it shifts the issue to the child's powerlessness.

Think of the many forms of commanding: scolding, nagging, screaming, threatening. The more we use these negative methods of pulling authority, the less effective we become as parents. The human spirit—even a child's spirit—longs for dignity and respect, along with simple love and affection. When denied these things, we rebel just as surely as the

American colonies rebelled when it became clear that the British would not respect their needs. The abuse of power creates the seed of rebellion.

The parent must be in control. Parents have a certain amount of power and authority, but (regardless of a common misconception) it is not an unlimited amount. In other words, children will respect power and authority, properly used, up to a certain limit. Think of it as a "bank account" of authority. If you invest too much of your account unpleasantly, you will have too little left to control your child's behavior in the long run. The older your child grows, the more binding this principle becomes. In our new world, we see parents expending their authority negatively and finding in the end that they have lost it and become helpless.

Pleasant but firm—that should be your motto. This approach conserves and enhances your authority, because you play to your child's respect rather than your child's helplessness. You sow love and respect, and you reap it in return. Your wrath is the point of greatest fear for your child because it draws your love into question and because it is threatening in and of itself. By respecting your child instead, you are

- Empowering him
- Giving him grounds for tremendous gratitude that will last throughout his life
- Increasing intimacy in your relationship
- Investing in the well-being of your grandchildren

The verbal element is a crucial backdrop for disciplinary issues. Choosing to be loving and positive makes a tremendous difference.

Gentle Physical Manipulation

Another positive tool for behavior control is gentle physical manipulation. It's very effective and highly recommended, not only for younger children but also for older ones at times.

An ideal example of this concept is the "no" stage that every two- to three-year-old passes through. You ask your child to come closer so your friend can see her. Of course she says, "No!"

This can be wearisome to parents, but we all know it's an absolutely normal developmental stage. So you use a request: "Amy, will you come over here and meet a nice new friend?" "No!" You shift to a command: "Amy, come here right now, please." "No, no!" Your temptation is to apply punishment, but there's a much better, more positive option: You gently usher her into place as requested.

This way Amy doesn't "win" or take control of the situation, but on the other hand she realizes you might have brought out all your heavy artillery and "been mean." She knows this is a test of wills. She knows that you have kept control of the situation, but gently and lovingly. Once again, the atmosphere of unconditional love has been maintained.

In addition, we have now moved through requests, commands, and gentle manipulation. It is now that we can clearly evaluate our child's behavior, for if this third and physical strategy is opposed, we know we are dealing with actual defiance in our child. We need to differentiate between *negativism*—which is simply the normal toddler stage of exploring independence and self-assertion—and the more serious *defiance*.

I suggest that you begin by giving your child the benefit of the doubt. Assume the more innocuous negativism until it becomes clear that your child is intent on rebellion. This way you keep everything positive and nonhurtful as long as possible.

Punishment

We now come to our fourth method for managing the child's behavior. Punishment is at once the most negative and the most difficult to administer.

Why? Four reasons:

1. Punishment must rigorously fit the crime; kids pay attention to fairness.
2. Punishment must fit the age level—so it must constantly be updated.
3. Punishments have different effects on different children: one hates time out in his room; another enjoys it.
4. Parents are inconsistent based on the mood of the moment.

As you can see (and as you probably know from experience), punishment is a great can of worms. Once it is opened, there are all kinds of issues that need to be addressed based on your child's age, your child's unique personality, your consistency, the subjectivity of fairness, and so on. The cliché "This is going to hurt me more than it hurts you" has some truth to it. We tend to agonize while our children are being punished, because there are so many gray areas and uncertainties. We wonder if we're being too strict and damaging our child or our relationship with him; we wonder if we're being too light; we wonder about the other siblings and whether we're showing favoritism or even being perceived as doing so.

Still, the time comes for punishment, as it does for these other approaches. The best way to face the issue of punishment is to think and plan ahead. Talk to your spouse, your own parents, or a good friend. Think about each child separately and what an appropriate punishment might be for a specific misbehavior (generally we can anticipate the kind of misbehavior we're likely to encounter). Write out your thoughts. The more advance preparation you apply, the more you build a protective hedge for your own anger at the future moment of the misbehavior—for one of the great problems about discipline is the way our own subjective emotions drive the episode.

Now the moment of misbehavior arrives. Quickly ask yourself the series of questions we discussed above: Is my child's emotional tank full? Is the problem physical? and so on. If all the answers are no and you have no success with the other and more positive methods of behavior control, you need to ask, Is my child actually being defiant?

Defiance is openly resisting and challenging parental authority, and of course that kind of behavior is not acceptable in your home. Your control must be maintained at all times. Your task is to break the defiance but to do it in the least damaging way possible. Another way to say this is that you want to make the least possible expenditure of your resource of authority. Remember, you have a certain amount of "authority capital," and it has spending limits. Punishment spends it very quickly.

Over the years I've observed how common it is for parents to overreact, using strict punishment and heavy authority on relatively minor and ordinary behavioral episodes—swatting flies with a baseball bat, as we might say. Later, when the more significant crises emerge, the parents have overspent their authority. If they had reacted with more measured discipline earlier, their children would now be identifying with them more closely, and the general atmosphere would be more conducive to the level of discipline that is now called for. Defiance, then, needs to be broken—but look before you leap. If your child feels unconditionally loved, the strategy of request or perhaps command may work. Let your child see that you would rather use the gentlest form of treatment.

Let me also observe that our kids often know us better emotionally than we know ourselves. They are very conscious of those moments when we have a choice between positive and negative approaches in dealing with them. They watch to see what the choice will be, and they draw conclusions about our own abilities to deal with our emotions. When we choose the high road, the children deeply appreciate it, though they may not demonstrate that appreciation. In using a positive approach, we have made an investment in greater respect from our children, and we've taught a lesson in solving problems positively.

A good (and misunderstood) scriptural concept for this attitude is meekness. In his Sermon on the Mount, Jesus said that the meek would inherit the earth (Matthew 5:5). That has nothing to do with shyness or timidity. It has to do with having yet restraining power. Jesus's listeners wanted a military leader who would raise an army to fight the Romans. They wanted raw, avenging power.

Yet Jesus told them that meekness (the base meaning for his term was "gentleness") is more effective in conquering the world. Power becomes more powerful when it is restrained. The gentle, Jesus taught, have faith rather than a quick trigger finger. They wait and trust God and—in the case of parenting—trust their children. Your children know what kind of power you have. When you refrain from using it, a message of tremendous power is sent and received—a message of love, trust, and respect.

Jesus himself, of course, had power that he used only for healing and for serving God. He held it in reserve, and therefore his authority (because he didn't squander it) was magnified (Philippians 2:6, 9).

He is our model in all things, and parenting is no exception. The two final and culminating fruits of the Spirit, as named by Paul, are gentleness and self-control (Galatians 5:23). When our children see us use these, our authority is increased. And more important, so are love, trust, respect, and identification.

To Spank or Not to Spank? There will always be controversy surrounding the form of discipline known as spanking. On balance, we must say that spanking has its good sides and its bad. On the good side, it certainly gets quick results, particularly in the case of young children. It is also quick and available at all times, requiring no thought or planning.

On the negative side, spanking grows less effective as the child grows older. It also decreases in power the more it is used. Overuse breeds all the negative emotions we have discussed in this book: resentment, bitterness, and antiauthority and antiparent mind-sets. Spanking lends itself a bit too well to the hot-tempered mood of the parent, and it moves perilously close to that line where abuse becomes an issue—and we know that abuse is as great an issue in our society as it has ever been. Some opponents argue that spanking simply reinforces the idea of violence in the child, and we can't simply ignore that possibility—not in a world of growing violence among young people.

While the physical pain of spanking may pass quickly, the emotional mark lasts a long time. It wasn't long ago that I talked with a man, nearly ninety years old, who admitted that he still suffered deeply over the memories of spankings in his childhood. Brutal spankings, of course, can be known by a more accurate name: *beatings*. They often cause terrible disruption in the mental and emotional life of a human being.

I have spoken to others who point to their own childhood spankings with a kind of pride—almost as a happy memory. These are the people who hold high the banner of corporal punishment. It is my theory that such people, though spanked, were greatly loved by their parents. There was a great abundance of positive nurture in the household. Emotional tanks were filled, and spanking became an extension of love.

But this is almost never the case in the new world before us. In past years, a harsher approach to discipline could work as long as a strong foundation of love was in place. I believe parents no longer have the same range of freedom if they want to raise positive, emotionally healthy children. What has changed? The social context. Nearly every cultural influence on the parent-child relationship is negative, enticing children to antiauthority, especially antiparent, attitudes. Therefore, discipline is riskier business than it has been in the past. Heavy punishment patterns can be devastating.

Children in general feel less loved in this new, hectic world for many reasons. Their parents are on the go all the time— they themselves are often just as busy—and with empty tanks, the spankings create much more resentment than training.

Let's remember that discipline and punishment are not the same. Discipline is training the child in the way he should go (Proverbs 22:6). The better disciplined (trained) your child is, the less punishment he needs.

But what about those three famous verses? Christian advocates of spanking often cite Proverbs 13:24; 23:13; and 29:15 to clinch their case. The first of these, for example, says, "He who spares the rod hates his son, but he who loves him is careful to discipline him."

What about that "rod"? Is it strictly an implement of thrashing? We often forget that it was most often used to guide sheep. The rod was held to gently block the sheep from wandering off in the wrong direction. It wasn't a tool for beating the sheep. After all, "Your rod and your staff, they comfort me" (Psalm 23:4).

At the same time, we may also overlook the countless biblical verses speaking of love, compassion, restraint, gentleness, grace, and avoiding the provocation of our children.

There are times we can effectively—and gently—use spanking as a last resort. I observed a wonderful example a few years ago in the life of my daughter, Carey. Her daughter Cami was only three at the time. Carey worked in the yard as Cami played nearby. Never had Mommy had to use corporal punishment up to this point. She had always found a more positive way to train her child. But today, despite warnings, Cami was interested in playing near or even in the street. Carey called to her, "Cami, could you please stay out of the street, dear? I don't want you to get hurt!" Obviously she used a request reflecting gentleness and love.

One moment later, Cami was testing the limits. She had wandered back into the street. Her mother used a command: "Cami! Come back here right now! I have asked you to stay out of the street."

For the third time, Cami wandered into the street, eying her mother warily. Firmly, she said, "I warned you to stay out of the street, and I meant every word." Now she used gentle physical manipulation, taking Cami's shoulders in her hands and leading her back to the safety of the front yard.

But Cami pushed the issue one step too far. When she ventured near the street again, she received her first spanking—"bottom-line" love. And the message certainly came across, for when Daddy arrived home and parked his car, Cami ran out to meet him. "Daddy! Don't run into the street!" she called urgently.

I'm proud of my daughter's well-trained training. She used all the right strategies in the right order and with the right result. Children can do well with or without spanking. The real issues are a loving household and emotional health and their impact on training.

Can you spank? Yes, if you do so wisely and as a last resort. But you're likely to discover that as you learn to employ positive strategies, spanking will no longer be an issue.

Behavior Modification

Behavior modification involves the use of positive and negative reinforcement to direct the behavior of a child. Desirable behavior is rewarded, while undesirable behavior is punished. We say that "B-mod" is neutral because the stimulus can be positive or negative. Technically this is true, but this "neutral" approach carries much negative baggage as the primary way of relating to a child. There are two looming problems:

1. It moves parent and child away from the pattern of unconditional love.
2. It moves the child toward a selfish orientation: "What's my reward?"

If you're going to use the reward-and-penalty techniques of behavior modification, you should use them very sparingly. If they come to dominate your relationship, your home will become a transaction-based setting where people serve one another not from love but from motives of profit or fear. We all know that this isn't the environment of love, caring, and nurture God designed the home to have.

On this matter of transactional or legalistic relationships, Paul wrote: "Let no debt remain outstanding, except the continuing debt to love one another" (Romans 13:8). In the next verses, he explained that all the commandments are summarized in the Great Commandment to love one another. Behavior modification is a very legalistic system that involves earning approval. Its very foundation is conditional approval. No matter how hard we try, we cannot frequently use it without sending a message that says, "I love you as long as you follow these rules."

At the same time, behavior modification deals completely with the symptoms of what is going on inside your child. It's like dealing with the sneeze rather than the flu that causes it. Your child's needs are primarily emotional, and the greatest need of all is unconditional love.

The new world is filled with "B-mod kids" who have become adults concerned not with values and integrity but with reward and penalty. Their training has been deflected from issues of the heart to the preeminence of *consequences*— the payoff, which is either the carrot or the electric shock, in lab terms.

We therefore have a generation, for example, that approves of income-tax cheating, as long as one isn't caught. Extra-marital affairs at work are seen as acceptable, for what the spouse doesn't know won't hurt him or her. We find that more of our kids are willing to cheat on tests—it's all about the consequence, and the consequence is getting an A, isn't it?

So when *can* we use the behavior modification method? It can be helpful in certain cases such as those involving

- Severe behavioral problems caused by sibling rivalry

- Specific, recurring behavioral problems when a child shows no remorse

- An early teen girl having communicational conflict with her mother

The third of those is a typical stage for many girls of that age. B-mod can be effectively used in such a situation. If you'd like to know more about how to use these techniques in specific situations, read Ruth Peters's book *Don't Be Afraid to Discipline.* She honestly admits to being a behaviorist and uses B-mod techniques carefully and in certain situations.

GUILT AND PUNISHMENT

When your child is truly sorry, rejoice! You want your child to develop a conscience, and in that regard, guilt is good. There's too little of it around these days.

An interesting phenomenon occurs when we punish our children—particularly when we spank. A child feels that the price of misbehavior has been paid and the slate is clean. In their eyes we're wiping away the guilt, and that may not always be a good thing. Once again, we see that a surplus of punishment removes that healthy level of guilt we all need to develop an inner moral and ethical system. We don't want our children to be guilt-ridden, but we do want them to develop a healthy conscience.

Pay attention to your child's level of remorse. It's very important. Some children will quickly say, "I'm sorry! I'm sorry!" simply to avoid punishment, and you can easily detect that motive. But if your child is deeply sorry, you can teach a powerful lesson by simply forgiving. Paul wrote about how to handle someone who has "caused grief." If the person is filled with sorrow, he suggests, no more punishment is needed: "Instead, you ought to forgive and comfort him, so that he will not be overwhelmed by excessive sorrow. I urge you, therefore, to reaffirm your love for him" (2 Corinthians 2:7–8). No greater advice could be given to a parent.

Forgiving a remorseful child is often the only way to train a child in this delicate, difficult art of forgiveness. Have you ever found you couldn't forgive yourself for something in the past? Have you realized you were unwilling to forgive a coworker or even a parent? We can't teach what we haven't learned. Be certain you truly forgive your child. This trains them to practice this precious art that separates Christianity from all other faiths.

Paul also wrote, "Be kind and compassionate to one another, forgiving each other, just as in Christ God forgave you" (Ephesians 4:32). This does not mean to ignore misbehavior. But when the right time comes, the sorrow is real, and the tears flow, hold your child to you and offer a love that overwhelms conflict. Teach your wayward child that final profound lesson—the lesson of the prodigal, which is perhaps the most profound of all. Demonstrate what it means to be cleanly, purely forgiven in a world of unconditional love.

4 THE POWER OF PROTECTION

THE MADISONS HAVE A VERY DEPENDABLE BABY-SITTER—
one who captivates their four-year-old son, Tyler. Zenith is
colorful, lively, and loaded with talent. She keeps Tyler enter-
tained with stories, songs, and humor. While Tyler is an active
child, he sits very quietly, his eyes alight, when Zenith is doing
her thing.

Zenith's greatest asset is her ability to teach, because she
makes it all fun and fascinating. She can tell Tyler all about the
world and how it works, bringing to life the sights, sounds,
and rhythms of people and places. Mr. and Mrs. Madison
don't always approve of her language, some of which is offensive. They try to keep her on "safe" topics, but they can't always
be around—that's why they use a baby-sitter in the first place.

The Madisons would be a bit more comfortable if Zenith
weren't so preoccupied with crime and violence. She is quite

devoted to it and quick to share all the details with little Tyler. Sometimes she shows him pictures filled with blood and death. By now, Tyler has seen so much of it that it doesn't really bother him much anymore. But he's been asking a lot of questions about sex for a four-year-old. That's another one of Zenith's special preoccupations—free, uninhibited sex of all kinds and with all sorts of people. She's more than willing to tell Tyler all about it.

Would you say that Zenith is less than ideal for the position of baby-sitter? I would, too, but the problem is, she plays that role in millions of homes. I often think it would be better if we unplugged her and put her out in the street! For Zenith, as you have guessed, is a television set. And while we have plenty of reason for concern over the place of television in the lives of our children, the fact is that it's only one of many influences that are targeting our children in this strange new world.

When a child begins life, his experiences are completely under the control of his parents. But with each year that goes by, his exposure to the world and its influences grows outward like concentric circles—like a pebble tossed into a quiet stream. In the first years of school, you experience some of your first concerns about the people and ideas he will see and hear. You will disapprove of many of the images and ideas that flash before his eyes on television or at the movies. But by the onset of the teenage years, media influences will seem much less dangerous than those of real life: peers, temptations, idle hours after school.

The world has always carried its quota of danger, but these times have dramatically altered the protective duty of parents. It's no longer the relatively safe world of our parents or grandparents. They didn't have to worry about metal detectors at elementary schools, terrorist acts in crowded places, or Internet pornography. Child and teenage peer groups contained far fewer troubled, angry children from confused or broken households.

We've seen that by far your most important task as a parent is to establish a home built on unconditional love. Then you must begin to train your child, using wise and gentle discipline. If you succeed at a high level in these goals, your children will survive the perils of a culture that is increasingly ethically and spiritually bankrupt. But even so, the challenges of that world must be faced. We may choose to homeschool, send our children to Christian academies, or simply immerse our lives in church activities. All these can provide positive, value-enriched experiences for our children.

But the fact remains that at some point our children, as they grow, must leave the cloister and engage the culture. And we know that the time also comes when we must acknowledge that our children, like their parents, are called by God to be the salt of the earth and the light of the world. Our faith is given to us not merely for defense but for going on the offensive. Your children, if you raise and prepare them well, will have a strong self-concept, bedrock integrity, and powerful faith values. They can do more than survive this hurting world— they can be part of the solution.

When times are dark, we need never lose hope. Look to your Lord as your children look to you. He will watch over your household. Trust him to provide the love, power, and security your home needs. Psalm 127:1–5 begins, "Unless the LORD builds the house, its builders labor in vain." Then, in the verses that follow, the psalmist compares our children to arrows in the warrior's quiver. We set our sights with care, we draw back the bowstring with all our strength, and we fire them into an always uncertain future. That's the long-term perspective of your God-given duty as a parent. Our children are the world's best hope for a peaceful and positive world tomorrow.

Therefore, we must be wary but not fearful. When we find ourselves in a frightening new world, we must move forward intelligently, with diligent preparedness. We have to be intentional about the security of our children. And even as we learn to think in a new way, it is just as crucial that we teach our children to do the same. Jesus sent out his disciples with these words: "I am sending you out like sheep among wolves. Therefore be as shrewd as snakes and as innocent as doves" (Matthew 10:16). Those words ring truer than ever in this present darkness. We need to be shrewd in the ways of the world, and we need to help our children be the same. Innocence is one thing, but naiveté is dangerous. Jesus tells us it's possible to be innocent yet wise; let's make that a goal in our parental training.

THINKING 101

You won't always be around to make decisions for your child. The time will come when he must discern what is the right thing to do. At that point, the question will be less about sheltering and more about training in right thinking. I set seventeen as the milestone age, your goal for a child's fully formed conscience and value system.

Therefore, on the one hand, yes, you definitely need to protect your child from harmful influences. But on the other hand, you need to find effective ways to discuss and to train. While you should be selective about the programs and movies that are viewed in your family room, you should also look for appropriate opportunities to discuss important issues. A movie might depict an improper relationship between a man and a woman. It's important not only to point out your disapproval but to explain *why.*

The reasons are very important to your children. You can say, "Because the Bible says so," only so often. They need to understand there are very valid reasons the Bible establishes limits and boundaries. At the same time, not every point of modern controversy is covered between those pages. Therefore, your children must be taught to *think* biblically, rather than to merely recite dogma.

As you make household decisions, discuss your thinking with your kids. Ask them about right and wrong behavior in their own world: cheating on tests, bullying, stealing, and so forth. In our times we have seen the growth of so-called "situation ethics"— the idea that there are no absolute rights or wrongs and that we're left to come up with our own value systems. This is really nothing new. Judges 21:25 describes a time when Israel lacked moral leadership, and "everyone did what was right in his own eyes" (NASB). A country is in great danger when its moral compass loses its true north and begins to spin out of control.

If there are no boundaries, nearly any kind of behavior can be rationalized. This is why your child needs a strong foundation of biblical truth combined with clear, value-based thinking to become a person of integrity. I believe integrity has three basic ingredients:

1. Telling the truth
2. Keeping promises
3. Taking responsibility for one's behavior

The Power of Protection

What about your own world? The people you know? The institutions with which you deal? I predict you've noticed the erosion of these three pillars of integrity in today's moral landscape. The world at large will not teach your child to honor truthfulness and commitment or to step up and take responsibility. These things must be taught, and taught well, in your home. We need to briefly consider each of these vital elements of integrity and explore approaches to instilling them in our children.

Telling the Truth

There was a time when we considered it sacred and binding to put one hand on a Bible and swear to tell the truth, the whole truth, and nothing but the truth. The symbolism of the act showed us that we bore witness not just before our community but before an all-seeing God who judges the deceitful.

Yet on that day several years ago when it became clear that our own president had lied under oath to a grand jury, many people were not particularly shocked; after all, they pointed out, we all tell "white lies." Wasn't President Clinton simply protecting his family and avoiding embarrassment? He actually provides a good example of the consequences of not training our children. Clinton's early family experiences, particularly with the lack of a father, failed him in the area of honesty. With all his personal intelligence and gifts, the lack of integrity left a deep stain on his legacy, the presidency, and our country's honor.

But he was only a symptom of a wider problem. *Reader's Digest* surveyed 2,624 readers on the subject of honesty. Here are the percentages of those who said they had . . .

- Called in sick at work when not ill: 63 percent

- Taken office supplies from their company for personal use: 63 percent

- Misstated facts on a résumé/job application: 18 percent

- Been undercharged/received too much change from a cashier and not told them: 50 percent

- Downloaded music from an Internet site without paying for it: 37 percent

- "Cheated" on their tax return (not declared income or overreported deductions): 17 percent

- Lied to their spouse about the cost of a recent purchase: 32 percent

- Lied to their spouse or partner about their relationship with another person: 28 percent[1]

The disruptive power of a lie cannot be overstated. A husband who lies to his wife forces a crack in the foundation of their marriage. A parent who lies to a child creates an atmosphere of distrust and insecurity. When we find we cannot believe in the most intimate relationships we have, there will be grave damage to our ability to trust anyone at all. And certainly our challenge to work together as a family toward the goals of growth and maturity will become steeper and more perilous.

Surely you've had this experience: Someone close to you lies, and you catch them at it. What is the effect on the future trust between you? How likely will you now be to tell this person something personal and important to you? Relationships are like ships: they are groups of people setting out on a journey together, and when the hull beneath their feet is breached, the ship cannot stay afloat. Honesty is among the deepest and most profound values your children must learn—and they must see it in practice for that lesson to prevail.

Keeping Promises

"I'll call you back tomorrow."

"The check is in the mail."

"I'll be out to fix your plumbing this week."

"In sickness and in health, for richer or poorer . . ."

Have you noticed the cheapening of commitment? Nothing seems permanent anymore, because we have become a fickle generation and we see no necessity in keeping our word. Even in our churches, new members stand before the congregation and commit themselves to the body of Christ—only to quickly transfer to another church when an exciting new pastor appears down the street. Businesses break their commitments to employees. Spouses desert their marriages and their children. Lewis Smedes wrote:

> Somewhere people still make and keep promises. They choose not to quit when the going gets rough because they promised once to see it through . . . I want to say to you that if you have a ship you will not desert, if you have people you will not forsake, if you have causes you will not abandon, then you are like God . . . With one simple word of promise, a person creates an island of certainty in a sea of uncertainty. When you make a promise, you take a hand in creating your own future.[2]

75

Failing to keep commitments creates havoc in society. An example can be found in the world of infant adoption. One of the reasons the process of adoption is so complex and difficult is that birth mothers often make legally binding promises, then switch gears and sue the adoptive parents. I know of a case where the adoptive parents have nearly been bankrupted by years of legal costs in protecting the child they brought into their home, the only home he has ever known.

We all know that financial promises (particularly among young couples) are far easier to make than to keep. We are overrun by foreclosures, repossessions, and unmanageable debt—which sends costs upward for the rest of us. Everyone makes a poor decision every now and then, and we all deserve a second chance. The problem is that so many people refuse to accept the consequences of their own ill-considered choices. If all or most people simply kept their basic promises, can you imagine the positive effect on our legal system?

Think about the business of promise-keeping in your family. If your child makes a commitment to some club or team, do you insist on his keeping his promise? If a child is allowed to take in a new pet on the condition that she feed it every day, do you see that she keeps her word?

At the same time, what about your own promises? Do you keep commitments at church? To your business? To your extended family? Is your family name established as a trust-worthy and dependable one in your community? Give it some thought. Your children are watching, and the standards you set are setting in. Particularly when you make a promise of any kind to your child—even if it seems like a small thing from your perspective—keep that commitment at all costs. If you forget, renege, or make some excuse, the message you are sending to your child is particularly poor. Not only are you breaking faith, but you are showing how important (or unimportant) your child and her world are to you.

Taking Responsibility

The blame game is as old as the Garden of Eden. After the first sin in the history of the world, God confronted Adam, who said, "The woman you put here with me—she gave me some fruit from the tree" (Genesis 3:12). God looked to Eve, and she pointed out, "The serpent deceived me" (3:13).

Only the serpent kept silent. He knew better than to pass off the blame before the searing gaze of God.

These days, it seems as if someone else is always to blame. We have become an incredibly litigious culture because the buck seems to stop . . . nowhere. If a crime is committed, it's society's fault. If a pastor is caught in moral compromise, the culprit is job stress. And we can blame nearly anything at all on some experience from our childhoods. Obviously, childhood training is important and does have consequences. But people are still responsible and accountable for their actions—or at least they should be.

The fastest-growing segment of law in America is the area of personal-injury lawsuits. And one of the latest trends is to sue fast-food restaurants as the cause of one's personal obesity. McDonald's, Pizza Hut, and other fast-food chains are actually paying large legal fees defending themselves from customers who simply walked in and ordered high-fat dinners. On March 10, 2004, the U.S. House of Representatives passed a bill known as the "Cheeseburger Bill" to throw out these suits. Yet there are countless other variations on the frivolous lawsuit clogging up our legal system and surely many more to come.

We all know what our kids say when we break up their argument. Each one quickly points at the other; it's always someone else's fault. We expect immature behavior from children. The problem is that we see so much of it in people who are thirty, forty, even fifty years of age or older. Have you ever apologized to your child, stepping up to take the blame for losing your temper or making the wrong decision? Hold yourself accountable—and allow others to hold you accountable—and you will teach a precious lesson.

On the day you see your child accept the consequences of his actions without argument, without blame, without excuses—then you've seen something all too rare in today's world. Think about the lessons of honesty, promise-keeping, and responsibility that are even now being taught in your home. What can you do to model a life of greater integrity? Let's think further about the process of passing on these values.

VALUES: MAKING THEM STICK

We all want our children to share our fundamental values in life. We want them to make our spiritual faith their own. We want them to discern what is right and what is wrong with the same mind-set we have. And for any child in this world, no one has a greater opportunity to make the difference than Mom or Dad. There will be other influences—friends, churches, schools, and simple personal reflection—but the parents are there first, during those years that are by far the most powerful in molding and shaping the human character.

This is one more example of the way we reflect the parenthood of our Lord, who similarly molds us. How so? Paul explained: "'Who has known the mind of the Lord that he may instruct him?' But we have the mind of Christ" (1 Corinthians 2:15). So we take on his mind, which really means his values and his way of thinking. This happens because each day, as his active followers, we "are being transformed into his likeness with ever-increasing glory, which comes from the Lord, who is the Spirit" (2 Corinthians 3:18). And so we strive to "be transformed by the renewing of [our minds]" (Romans 12:2).

This is what God, our heavenly Parent, has in mind for us: transformation to become more and more like him, to carry on his work in this world. Isn't that exactly what we have in mind for our own children? We want them to be like us, but even more like God. And to that end, we can spend countless hours and all the breath in our lungs verbally teaching them all these values. But how much of it will stick? We've all had the experience of speaking passionately about important things to our children, only to notice their attention wandering.

We need something more effective than talk. We need to mold our children's character as God molds ours: through *transformation*. We transform their lives by transforming their thought processes—the way they think, the way they see.

Before that can happen, of course, you need to be in touch with your own thinking processes. How are your own views shaped and conceptualized? What influences guide your conclusions? For each of us, the formula is a bit different—and frankly, for each of us there are unconscious factors that play a far greater role than we imagine in our decisions. But let's focus on conscious decision making: understanding how we think and how we transfer that process to our children.

"A Piece of Your Mind"

Have you given your children a good piece of your mind lately? Not in the way you may think—I'm referring to the process of explaining your thinking to your children.

Many parents, sadly enough, never let their children (or even their spouses) in on the details of their decision making. They lay out their conclusions and opinions but never the *why* part of things. In terms of the molding of our offspring, this is like telling them to go to another city but not giving them a map. If we don't explain how we got there, we shouldn't be surprised if our children eventually reject our ideas, beliefs, and values. The first step in teaching children to think is in teaching them how we think.

Make the word *because* an active part of your vocabulary, and make use of it when you state your decisions. It's not just for your children but for *you*—a means of reminding yourself of the good reasons that have motivated your decisions. Sometimes this stimulus may even spark you to think a little harder. Meanwhile, you'll be teaching your children to look at issues rationally, intelligently, and with good spiritual bearings. Your children will know your mind, and they'll be constantly developing mind-sets that bear your influence.

Being transparent and *articulate* about your feelings and motivations will help your child develop the same ability. I'm always surprised and disappointed to see how many parents raise children who lack the skills to identify and discuss their feelings—mainly because their parents haven't modeled that behavior. There are too many homes with little or no "emotional communication." Children don't know how or what their parents think and feel. Then the parents discover that they don't really understand the clusters of emotions, beliefs, and motivations that dwell inside their children.

When we understand our feelings, we are able to take them into account. As a simple example, if a man understands that he feels insecure around some of the more successful sales-people in his office, he will be able to identify his resentment and jealousy for what they are. Then he can detect when it is playing into his decisions in a destructive and/or self-destructive way. When a woman understands that she has unresolved feelings about her mother and the way she was raised, she can follow the way those feelings may creep into her adult life and impact present relationships.

Each of us carries a certain amount of old and new baggage with us, and the resulting emotions may fly beneath our own inner radar. So many of our actions and decisions are unduly influenced by these *unconscious* motivations, rather than by rational, logical, and faith-based thought. We want to "throw off everything that hinders and the sin that so easily entangles, and . . . run with perseverance the race marked out for us" (Hebrews 12:1). To do this, we must learn, and help our families learn, to throw off all those entangling influences that trip us up.

Through failing to clarify those issues or teach our children to do so, they in turn fail to learn to think logically. They will ultimately find themselves tripped up by "the sin that so easily entangles." And they may reach adulthood with no idea of how to manage their anger—or sometimes even no idea that they have a problem in that area.

The training we're talking about can't be done in an hour or two. It takes time and conscious effort. But every minute you put in now is an investment that will pay off tremendously in the future. An ounce of prevention now means many pounds of "cure" later on, during the years when unmanaged anger can damage your child's life.

Mind and Heart

Thinking and feeling are two separate issues that must always be considered. They are not the same. The average adult will tell you that he or she is a rational person, considering things logically and carefully before acting. But in truth, most of us are feelings-based movers. We are driven constantly by emotions of which we are half aware.

As a simple example, consider a conversation you might have with a specific friend—then with someone you may not even like. A conversation is filled with many little decisions as to what statement, observation, reaction, or question you will offer. Nearly everything you say is colored by your feelings—positive, negative, or ambivalent—about that person. A decision to volunteer (or not) for a committee at church may seem like a simple, straightforward matter of logical consideration. But when you stop to examine the dynamics of your decision, you will find a cluster of emotions about the church, your place in the church, the way you want to be seen, the person who is asking you, and other factors.

As a matter of fact, many churches are in turmoil today because of people driven by damaging emotions they don't understand. No one comes to the pew without bringing the emotional residue of Monday through Saturday, and a lot of aggression and passive aggression takes its toll in the sanctuary.

The truth is that unconscious motivations are the most powerful force in determining the course of a life. We may see ourselves as the "captains of our souls," but in fact there are clusters of feelings, positive and negative, that are moving us along. That is why there are times when we can't understand why we may or may not take certain actions. Why do we overeat? Why do certain kinds of people bother us so much? Why are we afraid to do this or that? Parents have the opportunity to make sure the right kinds of motivations fill their children—unconscious motivations to do positive things, to serve God, to make the world a better place.

Jesus once confronted a man who was literally swarming with inner demons. The man said, "My name is Legion . . . for we are many" (Mark 5:9). More often than we know, the inner urges and impulses that drive us are many. It's a little frightening to consider the power of emotions, but we need not live that life. We may choose to think and act logically—to manage our emotions so they don't manage us.

Let's think about how we can teach our children to master their emotions and live by unfettered logic.

Express Your Feelings with "I" Messages. It's always a good idea to express your feelings with "I" messages. For example, rather than saying, "I'm voting for Candidate A. He's the only choice in this election," say, "I agree with Candidate A's platform. In my opinion, he's the best choice on the ballot." You might then add the word *because* and give your reasons.

Why does this make a difference? You offer your statement as the way you think or feel, and you demonstrate your thinking process as well as your reasonable approach to it. You keep the conversation pleasant and nonpolarizing by presenting a basic humility. In the observation of your children, you're creating a model of reasonable, logical thinking based on compiled facts. You also avoid the implication that anyone else's opinion is unacceptable and will provoke an argument. Your children, then, have an open atmosphere to present and explore the thoughts and feelings you're encouraging them to examine.

We recognize, of course, that as emotional works in progress, children will often demonstrate raw, unreasonable perspectives. Your teenage son might say, "The teachers at my school stink. They all favor the girls and try their hardest to make the boys flunk out." Obviously that's an illogical statement—there's no need for you to dissect it on the spot and annoy your child. It makes much more sense to find any possible portion of your child's statement that you can agree with and acknowledge it as common ground. Then you can begin to ask good open-ended questions that will guide your teenager to examine the feelings that make him feel that way. In this case, perhaps you could say something like, "I've always felt that it's frustrating when someone doesn't give me the chance I deserve; do you feel the same way?" Then you might ask if there's been some fresh instance of this and why.

When we allow people to express their feelings, they'll often bring themselves to a more logical position. But when we start right in with corrections and contradictions, we create resentment and encourage them to entrench themselves in their irrational thoughts.

Disagree Gently and Patiently. Learning to think well is a journey. You can't instantaneously reach out and pluck them from their wrong position on the map and set them down at the right one. Instead, you need to gently point them down the right path, so that they can arrive at the goal of mature thinking themselves. Your child realizes that she doesn't have all the answers. She knows that she expresses a silly or unreasonable thought at times. Why draw undue attention to the fact? A good teacher knows how to motivate a student to reach for the right answer for herself.

Some parents are very impatient with their children's immature thinking. They're in a hurry for their fourteen-year-olds to think like forty-one-year-olds. Perhaps they've forgotten what it feels like in that perilous no man's land between childhood and adulthood. Do you wonder why teenagers suddenly clam up? There are several reasons, but one is that they need the freedom to "think out loud" without being frequently challenged. Most of us would feel the same way.

That's why you want to be gentle, open, and patient with your child's thinking. If you don't agree, you can still be agreeable. When your child discovers she has this freedom with you, there will be far more productive and enriching conversations. And as a consequence, your relationship will deepen and develop a more solid foundation. This is invaluable when the inevitable conflicts come. If you've established a bond of acceptance, gentleness, and patience, she will trust you to control yourself and to be an example of handling frustration during a disagreement. She will also feel that it's safe to come to you with a problem without your becoming disagreeable.

Let's apply these insights to the area of spiritual formation. If you present "I" messages ("I believe that God is . . ."), you present an openness and humility that are appealing to a younger person who is dealing with the questions that every human being faces as they mature. Many parents dogmatically hand out their religious beliefs to their children as if they were pills for instant faith. Spirituality, like other forms of thinking, is a journey that must ultimately be *personal,* though with the helpful and loving guidance of a parent or mentor pointing the way. It's reassuring for your child to know that you, too, have to work carefully through your faith.

Then, when your child has a question that might threaten or alarm some parents ("How do I know our faith is any better than Islam or Hinduism?"), you can be gentle and patient, with the results we've seen. Your child is most likely to abandon the faith teaching you provide if you create anger or resentment in him. One of the first targets for his rebellion will be in the area of faith. That's why it's all the more important that we be particularly open, loving, and patient as we help our children "continue to work out [their] salvation with fear and trembling, for it is God who works in [them] to will and to act according to his good purpose" (Philippians 2:12–13). (The "fear and trembling" refer to an awe and reverence that our children will begin to feel as they reflect for the very first time on the magnitude of these issues.)

Let's also consider the point that in this tense new world, depression and anxiety are soaring at unprecedented levels. Some experts project that one in eight teenagers may suffer from depression. The problem is that most parents don't know how to spot the symptoms. A 2002 study by Brown University showed that even parents who maintain good communication with their kids often fail to realize when their child is depressed.[3] Teens may turn to drugs less from peer pressure than from the need to find some relief from their unmanageable anxiety, and suicide among teenagers is a national epidemic. The very best opportunity parents have for helping their children is to leave doors wide open for gently, patiently sharing and accepting their children's thoughts and feelings.

The Power of Protection

PREPARING YOUR CHILD

Jeff's mommy had no clue how to tell him about the tonsillectomy he would undergo the next day at the hospital. So instead, she told him he was going to the zoo.

After the anesthetic wore off and Jeff woke up, he howled in pain and outrage for hours. His roommate, a boy named Charles, had a sore throat, too. But Charles also had a mother who had prepared him for the surgery. Now he sat and enjoyed his ice cream quietly.

Jeff is just one example of today's unprepared child. Parents aren't certain what to do or say in preparing their children for the bumps in the road. It can be a fine line; we don't want to overdo it, building our children's fear and uncertainty over rites of passage that lie years away. But in Jeff's case, for example, Mommy might have given him a big smile the day before the surgery, put him in the car, and driven him to the hospital to show him how impressive and interesting a hospital is. She could then explain the procedure and tell him that though his throat might be a little sore, there would be ice cream to make it better.

There's an old proverb that says the strong leader walks ahead of his people, walks beside them, and walks behind them. A parent needs to be one step ahead at all times. We need to anticipate the changes that lie ahead for the child, consider how encountering these changes might feel from the child's perspective, and then do what we can to help the child be ready. We provide the battle plans, the map, and the weapons—the battle is half won before our children march forward.

A classic example of the need for preparation is teenage

dating—especially for girls. A wise and loving father will take his daughter on "dates," showing her what it's like, how to behave in a restaurant, and so on. The daughter will then be calm and ready for what has been presented as a very pleasant and ordinary time. Of course, part of the preparation will have been a discussion of things that should *not* happen. The father will gently talk about how to handle these possibilities wisely and maturely. She'll know what to expect, what to do, and how to call her parents if necessary. The whole experience will feel less solitary and frightening.

We all know that this new world is sexually driven. We need to discuss this issue frankly with our kids. They will be confronted with immature and destructive sexual attitudes far earlier than their parents were. Because of the way the world has changed, we simply must be more open in discussing sexuality than our parents may have been. The more our children can explore their feelings in advance, under our gentle guidance, the more likely they are to choose the right (and logical) over the emotional thing to do. On the other hand, if we have not created the atmosphere of love and open discussion, we could drive our children to one more opportunity for rebellion.

We must discern the right timing. Rob, my editor, is raising his children in the Deep South. His children's school is very diverse racially. He watched with pleasure as his children worked and played from the beginning with children of various backgrounds. As they grew older and more sensitive to the differences and the tensions some children inherited from their parents, Rob found good opportunities to discuss race positively with his children. He gently prepared them for some of the racism and negative heritage they would inevitably notice and helped them formulate loving, accepting attitudes of equality on their own. Race is one more issue—one more new-world tension—we need to feel comfortable discussing with our children, so that we can prepare them to think and feel maturely as they become salt and light to this new world.

Violence, obscene language, anti-Christian attitudes—all of these are signs of the time. We need to notice them, see them as our children see them, and help them formulate their own thoughts.

The Teachable Moment

When you were in school, your teacher prepared you for tests. And if you were smart, you worked through your notes and assignments to prepare yourself. Then, when the test came, you knew you would make a good grade.

As parents, we are our children's teachers who need to get them ready for the tests they will face. We don't simply cross those bridges when we come to them, but we prepare carefully. This is why a good parent must be proactive—anticipating, adjusting, preparing, reviewing. We look just beyond the bend in the road to anticipate the test of potty training, the test of playing with other children, the test of attending school, the test of adolescence, and so on. In the beginning, you are your child's rock and fortress. Your new baby is totally helpless, and you provide complete protection. But the older your child grows, the more the protection shifts from you to the developing mind within your child. You can't sit beside your child in his seventh-grade class. You can't go on the first date or to summer camp.

As you prepare your child to make the right decisions himself, look for the teachable moments. These are those instants in time that seem tailor-made for your child to learn something important. There are two important kinds of teachable moments.

The first is the occasion when your child comes to you with a question. It's "teachable" because your child is interested; he has taken the initiative. No one learns without motivation to learn, so when these moments arrive, we need to seize the day. There are "why" periods when young children bombard you with questions. Rather than becoming irritated, realize that your child is hungry to learn. Never will he learn more effectively than right now. Many parents believe in giving their children "quality time," and that's good—but the questions may not arise during your designated period of "quality time."

The second powerful teachable moment comes when your child is connecting with you emotionally—a time when you are close and affectionate. An ideal example is bedtime. Many parents miss this golden opportunity because of television or other activities. Bedtime is a quiet, contemplative moment when your child loves for you to come sit on the bed and share a story, a devotional, or simply a good chat. I always enjoyed reading or making up stories that embodied a point I wanted my children to think about. We were delighted when they asked questions. These were like engraved invitations to come and teach their young and developing hearts and souls.

At bedtime, you can set the agenda for the thoughts that will occupy your children as they drift off to sleep. Ask them questions:

- What was your favorite moment today? Least favorite?

- Who do you know at school who is having a hard time and might need your help?

- What would be a nice thing to do at home tomorrow?

At bedtime in our home, we found opportunities to subtly mention difficult situations or issues that might lie ahead for our children. We were able to get the message across that they could come to us to talk about anything that might be on their minds.

LEARNING TO LET GO

We're all familiar with the word picture of the mother bird pushing her children out of the nest and forcing them to fly. We think about some day vaguely in the future, when our children pack their bags and leave our home. But in truth, as parents we are quietly releasing our grip a bit more each day from the time we bring them home from the hospital.

We let go a bit on the day we allow them to toddle through the family room without our hovering two feet away. We let go a little more on the day we allow them to cross a street to play with a neighborhood friend. We let go still more on the day they take the family car on a first date. Parenting is a sustained exercise in letting go—sometimes too subtle to notice, sometimes uneasy and painful.

So much of this ever-growing release is determined by our evaluation of the child's readiness. For example, different parents of sixteen-year-olds will have different comfort levels with handing the car keys to their teenagers. We vary even among our own children: One will be the "born responsible" type, ready to be trusted; another won't be ready at the same early age. How, then, do we handle the situation in which, for example, your son says, "How come I can't have the car tonight? You trusted my sister with it when she was my age."

The key is to be constantly educating our children about the consequences of behavior. Privileges, they need to see, are dependent on responsible behavior. Explain that the more mature a child shows herself to be, the greater the privileges she will earn. Once more, unconditional love decreases the tension in these situations. Your child knows he is loved, and he knows his parents want him to be happy. He will understand (even if he's impatient) that he has the opportunity to earn what he wants by proving himself trustworthy.

It's not always easy to set limits and keep them—it takes courage, as a matter of fact. The protection/release issue is a narrow tightrope every parent must walk. Your wisdom will be tested regularly, particularly when those teenage years arrive. Train your children from the beginning. Teach them to think logically and maturely, and show them your own thinking. They will disagree with your decisions at times, but if you have prepared them all along, they will ultimately respect your loving decisions—and in time, they will become the same kind of wise and loving parents.

5 DEFUSING THE ANGER EXPLOSION

A FAMILY IS A GARDEN—the wildest, most exotic and beautiful garden you will ever be given to tend. Each day we nurture what grows there. The right seeds must be planted, and the soil around them must be tended. All the right nutrients are essential, and there must be plenty of light and cool, refreshing water.

Since that day when the serpent slithered into the very first green sanctuary, we have faced a great problem with the gardens that constitute our families. Unhealthy contaminants are constantly seeping in, challenging all that we've planted and all that we envision in the way of fruit and blossom.

Alan Beck told about growing up in a rural community where tobacco was the chief crop. His first summer job was out in the field, weeding and hoeing row upon row. It wasn't too difficult to "scuff out" the weeds, he explains. But the closer he came to the fence, the more he ran into a certain variety of small thistles—hundreds and hundreds of them.

It was tempting to just let them lie; they were tiny, after all, and seemingly harmless. And the hoe was nearly useless to the task of scuffing them out. The thorough weeder, Beck said, had to stop, get down on his knees, and extract those prickly little thistles by the roots. And at the end of a long, sweaty day under the sun, that was the last thing he wanted to do.

But the experienced tobacco farmer knew that those thistles must be removed, as tiring and unpleasant and inconvenient as it seemed. Harvesttime was coming, and if the thistles remained, the farmer would reach down to get a handful of tobacco and come away with a palm full of thorns.[1]

In the garden of your family, you find thistles of your own—little irritants, points of frustration, unresolved conflicts. They may seem innocuous at the time. At the end of a long, hard day you may not want to deal with them. But it is my overwhelming experience as a counselor—and I expect it has also been your experience as a child, a friend, a spouse, and a parent —that those little thistles become thorns in time, and we're continually shocked and wounded by their sharpness.

Anger is a powerfully destructive force in our world today—an often unconscious determinant of a great deal of people's actions. How much anger is just beneath the placid surface of the average individual? You can find out by simply taking a drive in your car. Note the rage that quickly leaps out at the slightest provocation when people are behind the wheel, in a setting where they believe themselves to be anonymous.

Listen to the undertones of conversations around the water cooler: anger toward management; anger toward spouses; anger toward government, schools, communities. Young adults are finishing school, joining the work force, starting families, and already their psyches are permeated by anger. Why? Because anger comes with life, but it can and must be managed. Today, very few people have a clue how to do so. Their parents couldn't handle their own portion of it, and there was no way they could train their children. So their misguided techniques—venting, suppressing, or something else—have been passed on.

Let's state this fact very clearly: Training in anger management is the most crucial and difficult task that faces you as a parent. If you can successfully point the way toward healthy handling of anger, your child will be able to resolve most other problems as well; if not, nearly everything in life will be damaged by a rampant spirit of rage. I believe the thoughts and concepts of this chapter should be reviewed as constantly as you might take vitamins, clean the house, or get a medical checkup. Since anger is a constant force in our lives, it must be constantly and effectively confronted.

The Bible, of course, has it right: " 'In your anger do not sin': Do not let the sun go down while you are still angry, and do not give the devil a foothold" (Ephesians 4:26–27). Notice the powerful insights in this short passage that reassure us that the anger is not the sin; the misguided action that follows is what does the damage. Also, the power of anger increases exponentially as it ferments within us over time. That's the devil's foothold into your family's life.

Therefore, the time for defusing the anger explosion is always *now*.

RAPID RESPONSE

Anger is not only free of sin; in itself, it is useful and necessary to life. We read that God himself is angry at times. But anger can be a positive force only when it is handled in a positive way. And we all have seen the opposite: the disgrace of a furious parent shaking a small child, the boss throwing an ugly temper tantrum, even the husband striking his wife when an argument rages out of control.

Anger is a live wire within us; it subverts the circuits of logic and reasoning and fills us with the impulse to act irrationally. Later, we clean up the broken pieces of a relationship and ask ourselves, "What got into me? How could I say such a thing? How can I put this back together?" But as we know, a bell once rung cannot be unrung. Evil words cannot be taken back. The damage is immediate and often long-lasting. Thus we need to know how to manage our anger and to do so readily.

We have two anger responses: word and action. A young child, verbally less articulate, is nearly limited to behavior. But either way, we find both manifestations of anger unpleasant. Crying or whining, throwing toys, tantrums—these behaviors are irksome to us, and we want to stifle them immediately. If the child talks back, we focus on disrespect (a secondary issue) rather than the greater issue of anger. "Don't you talk back to me!" we shout, actually reinforcing the child's anger impulse by demonstrating it ourselves.

Most often we attempt to push the anger back inside our children. We don't want the noise; we don't want the words or the demonstrations. And the child, who has a powerful impulse that needs expression and who is too immature to master the art of self-control, must struggle to do what is very difficult even for adults. In any case, that anger cannot stay inside forever. It will find its way out somehow and in a new and more damaging form by this time. The longer it is held inside, the more irrational it becomes. Those who bottle up their anger suffer from every variety of neurosis or mental illness.

Anger, then, demands your attention and demands it *now*.

Defusing the Anger Explosion

I feel deeply for every single parent facing this dilemma. Realizing the true nature of the challenge facing your child— the difficult challenge of handling anger—there is even more pressure on you, the parent, to do the right thing. Sometimes your energy resources are low. Sometimes there are other issues and crises at the forefront of your mind. Yet here is this problem that must be faced, must be faced now, and must be faced wisely and patiently.

Before you can ever train your child to handle these moments correctly, you will need to train your own "rapid-response" mechanisms. It takes understanding the dynamics of your child and her emotions and maintaining a commitment to make anger training a top priority at every moment when it arises.

A CITY BENEATH THE CITY

The very first area we need to understand is the blueprint of how people are put together emotionally. As human beings we are tremendously complex. God created our "inmost being," and we are "fearfully and wonderfully made" (Psalm 139:13, 14). We know more than we did when the Psalms were written, yet there is still much that puzzles us about what makes us think, feel, and behave as we do.

When considering the complexity of the human soul, it's helpful to envision a large, thriving city. As a complex, multifaceted organism, you are like that city. On the outside, the metropolis is an impressive skyline of gleaming towers, humming with the pace of daily business, culture, religion, society. Beneath the facade, however, there are hidden systems that help the city run: pipes, wires, cables, drainage canals, a whole network of sewers beneath the streets. There are also men and women who make up the political matrix. They initiate deals, handle transactions, and impact the fate of the city in a quiet way.

Your emotional life is also composed of these outer/inner, visible/hidden layers of vigorous activity. At any given moment, your conscious mind is on one subject or another. If I offered you "a penny for your thoughts," you would tell me just what you happened to be considering at the time. But beneath the "streets" of those known thoughts, there are other mental and emotional activities, developments, and transactions. We call these the *unconscious* portions of the mind and personality.

Consider a topic such as, say, Christmas. As soon as I mention the word, the inner and the outer meanings come into play. Many of us have deep, often sentimental feelings about Christmas for reasons both conscious and unconscious. On the surface, you may think of shopping to be done, relatives to host, and decorations to make. But there are other associations and stimuli involved, too—how Christmas has made you feel in the past, memories of good food or favorite gifts, aromas, and feelings of security (or perhaps, for some people, loneliness or other negatives).

The important insight is this: We are filled with hidden complexes of emotion and perception. Just as the urban business day is largely determined by a hidden network of activity and transactions, many of your thoughts and feelings are similarly shaped *beneath the surface* of your conscious thoughts and mental transactions.

As a matter of fact, far more of our decisions are based on unconscious factors than we realize. Most of us believe ourselves to be very rational and objective people with unclouded minds, making our decisions based on purely impartial considerations. The truth is that our hidden (unconscious) influences provide much of the "wiring and plumbing" that push us toward our decisions and actions. No one emerges from their formative years with completely resolved feelings about the important issues. We have unfinished business concerning our parents, our siblings, our social standing, our self-worth, our sexuality, and religious issues. All of these networks of belief and emotion and impression actively run their circuits within us and help to shape us into the complex people that we are.

It's interesting to discover the same analogy in the Old Testament: "Like a city whose walls are broken down is a man who lacks self-control" (Proverbs 25:28). Training our children in anger management is, among other things, teaching the art of self-control.

THE PUNISHMENT TRAP

Now perhaps we can understand the dangers of the "punishment trap." Many parents believe that punishment is the best way to teach anger management. When they observe the symptoms of anger in word or deed, they quickly level the penalty. Surely, they reason, this will condition their children to control themselves simply to avoid punishment.

But this is a faulty perception, because it doesn't take into consideration the complexity of what lies within that child, beneath the surface. If your child begins repressing his anger simply to avoid the punishment, the "surface" of his personal cityscape may seem placid—but the anger does not go away. It is simply redirected through the inner workings of the child. If the anger is handled effectively—in a timely manner on the surface—it will be defused and go away. But if it is suppressed or repressed, it will take on a life of its own, deep within the hidden thoughts and feelings of the child. And you can expect it to reemerge later in a much more damaging way.

Let's take a more concrete example. Joey wants dinner at his favorite fast-food restaurant, but you're planning to cook. He expresses his disappointment, then begins to whine. He kicks the foot of the sofa. "Just stop it," you say, busy with your recipes. The whining increases in intensity. "You never listen to me," Joey accuses. "We never eat where I want to eat." You're at your wit's end, and you warn him that if he says another word about it, he can't watch television for twenty-four hours.

Joey doesn't want to lose TV privileges, and he sulks sullenly out of the room. But the frustration over the trivial matter goes unchecked. It sinks down into that network of raw emotions and unfinished business that lies far beneath the surface. Even though the dispute is a small matter, it is one to add to many others in Joey's developing personality. If he doesn't learn to handle his anger, and if you don't help him face the specific issues involved, these smaller issues will ball up inside. They will seep out later in the form of angry, problem-based behavior that will be much more difficult to handle.

There is another grave danger. As we've noted, many parents haven't been trained to handle their own anger. When their children push the wrong buttons, the parents dump all their own angry emotions on their children. The message they send is this: "You *will not* be allowed to express your anger. I will express *mine,* however—in an immature fashion and all over you!" Needless to say, we're teaching all the wrong lessons when this occurs. The child is helpless, defenseless—and at the moment, very angry.

That's a forlorn place to be, and let me make one more

point about the parent's own anger. I realize how difficult it is for us to control our own tempers in the context of parenting; there are so many moments in which we ourselves are deeply frustrated, seemingly pushed to the very edge of our patience. Our children know how to push those buttons, and sometimes it seems to us as if they are willfully pushing them on purpose. A recent article in the *New York Times* showed a study indicating a great majority of parents admit to losing their tempers with their children.

As common as it may be for parents to "blow their stack," we need to realize the consequences. *The most certain way to invite passive-aggressive or stealth anger in a child is to dump our own anger on them,* for nothing causes deeper resentment and frustration. Stealth anger will be considered over the next few pages.

One effective way to keep your own anger under control is to keep a journal. Write down your thoughts and frustrations at the end of each day—recording them is a good way to "bring them out into the light," to get an objective snapshot of your emotions. Review what you've written each day, and make new determinations about how you can handle things. This in itself will often defuse the worst of it.

Talking about those feelings with your spouse (not in the presence of your children) can also be a good way to deal with your own emotions without venting them on your child. But I hope you'll consider a daily parenting journal—you'll be amazed by how much it will help you sort out your emotions.

As for our children, how can we handle angry confrontations with them? What are the right responses when they display their anger? How can we handle it immediately and on the surface to avoid the punishment trap that sends anger deep within our children to do its damage?

In the next section, we'll see some practical steps that can be taken.

Right Response

1. Prepare in Times of Peace. The first and by far most crucial step you should take is to perform preventive maintenance. Be proactive during the nonangry moments in preparing your child for the more challenging times. You do this simply by keeping your child's emotional tank full. Yes, it sounds simple, and we've already gone over it—but the importance cannot be overstated. *A well-loved child will always be easier to handle than a child who doesn't feel loved.* If there is plenty of unconditional love and acceptance, you've created a positive atmosphere that will automatically defuse many of the tense moments. And your child will be dealing from a point of strength, rather than one of insecurity, when he comes to those points of conflict. He will know he is loved, and it will be easier to accept the conditions upon which you insist.

2. Take Hold of Perspective. Remember that "this is as bad as it gets." That is, teaching anger management is the hardest part of parenting. It shows the most unpleasant side of your child, and it plays to a personal weakness—your own anger. But remind yourself that your child is just that—a child—and is going to handle anger in an immature way. You will expect it to happen, you'll be ready, and you'll know that if you can make the best of these opportunities, you will have accomplished the hardest part of your mission. And you'll have prepared your child to be happy and successful in life. Tell yourself, "This is going to be unpleasant, but if I can handle these moments, I can handle any part of parenting. Bad things can happen, but that means good things can happen, too—I can turn these moments of crisis into moments of growth and maturity."

3. Encourage Verbalization. We know by now that the anger must be handled; that is, it must be expressed. It must not be suppressed. It can take two forms—word and action. The first is obviously the preferable, so encourage your child to verbalize her anger. If the anger can find its form in words, it will never need to be acted out.

The goal for expression of anger is very clear. I have always set it forth with this ascending scale. These conditions become a little more difficult as you move through the list. But when we master them all, we know we have learned to manage anger.

Handle your anger:

- Verbally

- Pleasantly

- By resolving it with the person with whom you're angry

- By finding ways to resolve it within yourself

At the very beginning, your child will handle anger verbally but unpleasantly. None of us enjoy whining, complaining, or other negative tones. But it's far better that you put up with a moment or two of unpleasantness than push the anger back within your child, where it will later choose the behavioral form of expression. If you have to deal with your child's anger, deal with it this way and work toward the next goal of a more pleasant transaction—and remember to avoid the trap of becoming angry yourself due to your child's unpleasant tone.

While you're doing the "dirty work" of listening to your

angry child, simply remember that you're avoiding a great deal of dirty work within her. An ounce of prevention is worth many pounds of cure in this situation. You're teaching your child that when she is angry, the right way to handle it is to bring that anger to you and resolve the issue now, *in words*. In time, she will resolve it more pleasantly; and eventually she will have the skills to work out her anger within in a positive way—and what a profound difference that will make in her life.

STEALTH ANGER

Suppressed anger sinks deep within us and does serious damage. We like to tell ourselves that when we stifle someone's anger, it will "cool down" and melt away. That's simply not the way emotions work. Unexpressed anger lives on to fight another day. Deprived of direct expression, it seeks a subtler outlet. Counselors call this *passive-aggressive* behavior, but that term has inspired a lot of misunderstanding. For the purpose of this book, let's refer to it as *stealth anger*.

In simplest terms, think of it this way. We all know that anger is a potent emotional force. It wants to be free, and its first impulse is to express itself directly. When your child is angry, you know it immediately—the anger is expressing itself directly. But what happens when we block the primary outlets? We repel them through unpleasant punishment and discipline. The anger, therefore, will not spring out as it would like, because the repercussions would be unpleasant. So it goes "underground," lurking in the complex network beneath that human structure that is so much like a city. It remains there and seeks a new and often stronger form of expression.

Defusing the Anger Explosion

There are a great number of reasons this is the worst of all options. For one thing, words are less troublesome than actions. But when the verbal path is blocked, anger will come out in behavior, and it will choose its own time. And that expression will be puzzling because it will be *irrational.* That is, we won't immediately see through to the true cause of the behavior—and generally, neither will the angry person.

Kelly is very angry about some issues at home, but her parents don't want to hear about it. They tell her to stop whining and solve her own problems. So Kelly has no verbal outlet for her feelings. In time, her grades begin to drop. Her parents are puzzled; she doesn't know the reason herself. Her anger is reemerging in a behavioral form and one much more damaging than her whining.

The problem, of course, is that Kelly needed a little attention. She needed to talk about these issues at home. When she wasn't granted that attention, she unconsciously began to manipulate her parents through her grades—something she knew they cared about. Stealth anger is very manipulative, and it is also retaliatory. It seeks to strike back at the person who is the object of the anger. Once Kelly's parents realize this, however, they would be terribly wrong to think Kelly did any of this on purpose. Again, these are actions that come from the "underground" of our personalities.

Stealth anger, then, is irrational and manipulative. It is stubborn, vicious, and far-reaching. It is also all around us in this new world of ours. Every parent will cope with a certain amount of stealth anger, but when it becomes the primary way our children handle anger, there will be great distress in a family.

Signals of Stealth Anger

How can you be certain you're dealing with this form of anger? Look for three primary signals:

1. *It is irrational.* Your child's particular actions make no sense. He does the very opposite of what you expect.

2. *It is unmanageable.* You will make all the obvious attempts to "fix" the behavior—yet nothing works. The behavior only becomes more stubborn, more irrational.

3. *It is self-inflicted.* The child is the one most damaged by his own behavior. Even when this becomes evident, the child will continue to inflict self-punishment through irrational, anger-driven behavior.

A sudden decline in grades, of course, is a classic expression of stealth anger because parents carry such an obvious interest in their children's schoolwork. Refusing to participate in church activities would be another one, particularly for older children. Your teenager may thrive on his involvement in the youth group, but suddenly she will refuse to be a part of it. Why? She is angry not at the church, not at God, but at something else usually in the home.

Ordinary Versus Serious Stealth Anger

Between ages thirteen and fifteen, the period we know as early adolescence, stealth anger or passive-aggressive anger is relatively normal. Even then, it shouldn't actually be harmful to anyone—otherwise, we cannot call it normal. Younger teens go through a difficult period, a rite of passage between childhood and adulthood. Many things in their world are changing, and emotions run high. As they learn to deal with anger during this stressful time, there will be a certain amount of stealthful, misdirected anger. But we must use these occasions to help them handle their anger in a more mature fashion. If they carry stealth anger into adulthood, they will do great harm to themselves as well as to others.

Following are some examples of actions or behaviors resulting from ordinary anger versus those resulting from stealth anger:

Ordinary	Serious
A stubbornly messy room	Experimentation with drugs
A slightly tougher time with grades	A sudden pattern of Fs
A new insistence on privacy; reluctance to talk	Active disobedience

In our new world, the problem of stealth anger and the risks associated with it are escalated because the weapons have become sharper. There were simply fewer ways for an angry young person to act out his frustration forty years ago. Today, there are widespread drugs, easier access to sexual activity and crime, and more cultural encouragement to rebel—even to the point of suicide. What this means is that your child's voyage will send him out to navigate the normal rocks and reefs, but he will do so on far choppier, more turbulent waves. It is crucial that you sit beside him on the voyage, listening carefully, reassuring him of his self-worth, and especially expressing your love and support at every opportunity.

As long as this time of life promises to be a roller coaster ride, the best thing a parent can do is to make the best of it. Encourage biking trips, ropes courses, and physical activities that appeal so much to the energy and overactive adrenaline of the teenager. Find activities and items that you can endorse, instead of simply those you must forbid—remembering, of course, that your child will look for places to set his *own* seal. For example, he may *need* to enjoy a certain style of music that he knows you can't handle; it helps set his own unique identity, which is the nature of this stage of life.

SWEET SEVENTEEN

Through my own observation, I've come to the conclusion that an appropriate goal for maturity is the seventeenth birthday. By the time your child reaches that point in time, he or she should know how to handle anger maturely. The sad truth is that this isn't the norm. Our world is filled with adults who have never learned to handle their anger. They are bringing stealth anger into the work force, into church, and of course into their own families. The result is a string of problems, disruptions, and broken relationships left in the wake of these frustrated individuals.

I've also used the concept of the "Anger Ladder" over the years. It helps demonstrate the full spectrum of responses to anger, from the worst (stealth or passive-aggressive anger) to the most mature behavior (pleasant, verbal, resolution-based communication). Studying the anger ladder will help you understand that your child is not born at the top, nor even in the

POSITIVE

1. Pleasant • Seeking resolution • Focusing anger on source • Holding to primary complaint • Thinking logically
2. Pleasant • Focusing anger on source • Holding to primary complaint • Thinking logically

POSITIVE AND NEGATIVE

3. Focusing anger on source • Holding to primary complaint • Thinking logically • Unpleasant, loud
4. Holding to primary complaint • Thinking logically • Unpleasant, loud • Displacing anger to other sources
5. Focusing anger on source • Holding to primary complaint • Thinking logically • Unpleasant, loud • Verbal abuse
6. Thinking logically • Unpleasant, loud • Displacing anger to other sources • Expressing unrelated complaints

PRIMARILY NEGATIVE

7. Unpleasant, loud • Displacing anger to other sources • Expressing unrelated complaints • Emotionally destructive behavior
8. Unpleasant, loud • Displacing anger to other sources • Expressing unrelated complaints • Verbal abuse • Emotionally destructive behavior
9. Unpleasant, loud • Cursing • Displacing anger to other sources • Expressing unrelated complaints • Verbal abuse • Emotionally destructive behavior
10. Focusing anger on source • Unpleasant, loud • Cursing • Displacing anger to other sources • Throwing objects • Emotionally destructive behavior
11. Unpleasant, loud • Cursing • Displacing anger to other sources • Throwing objects • Emotionally destructive behavior

NEGATIVE

12. Focusing anger on source • Unpleasant, loud • Cursing • Destroying property • Verbal abuse • Emotionally destructive behavior
13. Unpleasant, loud • Cursing • Displacing anger to other sources • Destroying property • Verbal abuse • Emotionally destructive behavior
14. Unpleasant, loud • Cursing • Displacing anger to other sources • Destroying property • Verbal abuse • Physical abuse • Emotionally destructive behavior
15. Passive-aggressive behavior

middle. She has to climb it rung by rung, moving from the most immature responses to (with your help) more and more positive ways to handle her anger. For example, you can't look for much progress before the age of six. Prior to that age, the main thing is to help her express her anger verbally and keep her from "going underground" with it and ultimately expressing it stealthfully and through behavior. Polish the ladder at all times through pouring unconditional love into your child. The more you share, the quicker your child will climb.

Also remember that your child may move down a rung or two—don't panic. This happens at the preteen age we've already discussed, when your child may begin to exert a certain amount of ordinary stealth anger. This is a particularly crucial time to listen, to love, and to have a good understanding of your child's whole emotional world. Where is the anger? How can it be better handled? As you deal with it rightly, you'll be teaching your child a more mature approach.

CARING FOR YOURSELF

It's also important to take inventory of your own issues as you deal with those of your children. What are you angry about? You may simply be angry that your child is angry—or it could be something from your own world. Look at that ladder again, from your own perspective rather than that of your child. Be certain you're dealing with your own emotions in a mature way. Talk it through with your spouse or trusted friend. Make a resolution that your own anger will not seep through into those fragile, crucial moments when you are working with your child.

Also, use self-talk. It's a great way to avoid reacting to unpleasant remarks from your child. There will be times when you have to listen to such verbalizations, because a child must be verbally unpleasant before he climbs up to that desired and preferable level of being pleasantly verbal. And the only alternative is to drive the anger underground by stifling it. Don't do that!

Here's what I mean by self-talk. You might go off to the side and tell yourself:

> I'm not going to let my child's anger get the better of me! Hey, I'm bigger than this. If it's the last thing I do, I'm going to prove I'm tougher than a few harsh words from one of my own children. I know I love my child, and I'm going to handle it with love instead of striking back.

Here's another example:

> This is not about me! It's just a normal part of growing up for my child. I know he loves me. I know I love him. Therefore, why should I be threatened by a turbulent moment or two? It takes a little fire to temper steel, and it takes a few heated moments for my child to learn to handle anger. This is pretty important, so instead of letting it get to me, I'm going to turn up the love even more.

Or:

> You can't fool me! I know this is a good rather than a bad thing. My child is bringing her anger to me. I would certainly rather have her do that than take it somewhere else, outside the home. She is putting a fantastic teaching opportunity right here in my lap!

Or:

I will absolutely not dump my own anger on this child, because I know that's the recipe for the kind of stealth anger that could totally disrupt her life. Every ounce of self-control I can produce now is a pound of prevention for her future—and I certainly love her strongly enough to give a couple of ounces of self-prevention.

One more good one:

Love is patient, love is kind . . . It is not rude, it is not self-seeking, it is not easily angered, it keeps no record of wrongs . . . It always protects, always trusts, always hopes, always perseveres. Love never fails. (1 Corinthians 13:4–5, 7–8)

That last one, of course, reminds us that as parents and as people, we have the most infinite of resources available to us. We know that "the fruit of the Spirit is love, joy, peace, patience, kindness, goodness, faithfulness, gentleness and self-control" (Galatians 5:22–23). All of those wonderful attributes are the result of trusting God more fully with the everyday cares of life. That last one, self-control, will be particularly helpful to you during parenting's greatest trials. In those moments when parenting seems all but impossible, when you feel overwhelmed, and when you feel as if you've come to your wit's end—simply bow before God, acknowledge that he has the wisdom and the way that you need, and trust him to give you peace and victory.

I would also suggest that you select any self-talk statements above that you find helpful and copy them onto five-by-seven note cards. Keep them in your pocket during the tough times, and go over them regularly, speaking them to yourself. The more you build them into your outlook, the more you will make use of these powerful truths during the moment of truth.

STEPS TOWARD THE TEACHABLE MOMENT

Remember This Policy: Patient but Firm

Patient but firm should be your approach at all times as you deal with your child who is verbalizing his anger. While you are allowing him to talk about his anger, you are *not* allowing him to control the terms of the encounter, and you are *not* allowing him to use the occasion to manipulate you in any way. Listen and love, but set your policies and maintain them consistently.

Keep It Calm

When your child brings you her anger, she is bringing herself to be taught. And as we have suggested, *now* is the best time for that lesson. But if you or your child is overwrought, those high emotions will prove counterproductive. Make it clear that you want to talk about the problem, but that it would be a good idea to take at least a few minutes until the emotional barometer level drops.

Don't Condemn

Let your child know immediately that there will be no condemnation. He knows he is angry, and he probably feels some guilt already. Remember the importance of unconditional love. It is at these times above all others when our children need to be reminded that nothing can prevent our love for them. Your child is accepted, your child's feelings are accepted, and his verbal expression of them is also accepted. Make those conditions clear, so the door will be open toward resolution.

Find the Positive Things Your Child Did

If your child has brought you her anger, that's a positive development in itself. If your child hasn't acted out her anger—slamming doors, venting her rage, or insulting someone—you have at least some grounds for commendation. Again, you are underlining your love and support, even in conflict, and laying the groundwork for a positive resolution.

Point to a Better Way

Finally, having listened, having reviewed, having allowed your child to verbalize his anger, you have that brief and wonderful moment in which training is possible. Point out a better way for your child to handle his anger next time. Offer him the next rung on the anger ladder. This episode could have been worse, but it could be better, too—and next time you'll be pleased to see a glimmer of progress toward maturity, as your child moves upward toward a better way.

FINALLY, FORGIVENESS

Let's close this important chapter with a few words on the power of forgiveness. Nothing is more basic to our spiritual faith than this concept, for we know that God has already forgiven us for every transgression. Though we continue to live imperfectly, stumbling as we go, the basis of our belief is that he looks on us and sees only the perfection of Jesus Christ, his Son. The word for that is *grace,* and we live every moment in the wonders of that grace. I've often said that *forgiveness is giving up the right to get even.*

We must pass forgiveness on to our children, so that they may learn to live the same way. The climb toward emotional maturity for our children will be a bumpy one. They will make many mistakes. At times they may plunge several rungs down the ladder. It must be very clear to them at all times that they are forgiven and that forgiveness has no limit.

But we aren't speaking only of forgiving them. We, too, need to be forgiven. Many parents have never apologized to their children for speaking too crossly to them, for unloading some of their own rage on them, for failing to give them the moment of attention they needed. It's so important for us to show our children that we realize we aren't perfect and that we need their forgiveness as much as they need ours. Otherwise it seems to be a very unfair, one-sided world they live in, filled with double standards. But when we approach them on the basis of apology and seeking forgiveness, we show them a deep respect that they acknowledge and welcome. We grant them true personhood. We show them we consider them already to be the mature individuals we are guiding them toward becoming.

There's nothing wrong with telling your children, "If you ever feel that I treat you unfairly—if you ever feel that I truly wrong you in some way—I want you to come to me immediately, and we'll talk about it." Your child may take up that invitation, and you should be prepared to objectively consider what is brought to you. If such hearings are held two or three times in a year, that's a good sign. Your children are airing their concerns; they're far weaker candidates for actions of stealth anger. And your children will respond positively to being treated in a mature way. You will feel greater closeness to them as a result.

At the end of the day, we reflect sadly over the power of anger in our world and in our homes. It is a turbulent storm that seems to rip through whole societies of people around us, leaving devastation in its wake. It ruins businesses, churches, governments, and whole communities.

Yet forgiveness is even more powerful, because there is no transgression in all this world that cannot be trumped by forgiveness. Our Lord has already proved that fact for all eternity. Along with all the hours and the blood, the sweat, and the tears of bearing up your children toward the high goal of emotional maturity, perhaps the greatest lesson of all will come in that moment when they stand quietly in the background and watch you forgive. They see your tears as you embrace the neighbor, coworker, adult sibling, parent, pastor, or perhaps the spouse who had previously filled you with rage.

For in the home, younger ears are always listening. They are specially tuned in to the anger of parents, even as they wrestle with it themselves. If you can find no victory over your anger, then your teaching lesson will be a difficult one indeed. One action, one attitude on your part, can undermine one thousand good words of teaching.

But the reverse is also true. When your children see the power of forgiveness in your life, they will be reaching for the next rung without even realizing it.

6 CONFRONTING THE MEDIA MONSTER

I HEARD THE STORY OF A SINGLE MAN who bought a beautiful canary to add color and music to his parlor. From within its cage, the canary sang all day long. The melody was pleasant, bringing great joy to the little bird's owner.

One day he had the thought of giving his little canary some fresh air. So he took the little cage out to his backyard and delicately hung it on the branch of a tree. The canary was quiet at first, suspicious of her new surroundings. But after a few minutes she began to sing, and a few other birds perched nearby. Most of these were sparrows, and they chirped in their own more common voice.

The man made this a habit, letting his canary enjoy the morning while he went about his daily chores each day. But far too soon, he noticed something new and disappointing about his pet. The canary's beautiful song had disappeared. The little bird now possessed only the common, tuneless call of the sparrow. She had been too long among the sparrows and crows, and her song had become coarse and unappealing.

As parents, we can almost *feel* that day when our "canaries" first encounter the "sparrows." Our toddlers are captive audiences, fully in our care and happy with the simple toys we've provided them or perhaps with a well-produced television show or video created specially for that age. The lovely, unspoiled innocence of our little children is as pure as the canary's song. But we know that times will change. Someday, we'll no longer be able to monitor each moment in the lives of our children.

Parenting is the progressive act of letting go; even canaries must finally leave the nest to fly and to sing their own unique song. Our children will come under many new kinds of influences. Some of these—school, church, Scouting, or clubs—are wholesome and even necessary. After all, your child could never become a complete and healthy individual without the spectrum of other relationships and group identities that bring their own distinctive contributions.

But times have changed. It is as if the jungle has encroached rapidly upon the mission settlement these past three or four decades; the sparrows and the crows are dominating the "soundscape." We look out on this world and wonder how the sacred became the profane. An increasingly wayward and rebellious culture seeks to reach into our living rooms and claim our children.

A study by the Center for Media and Public Affairs compared the views of Hollywood's TV writers and executives with those of mainstream America on several subjects. Results:

- *Adultery:* wrong for 85 percent of mainstreamers; only 49 percent of the TV crowd agree.

- *Abortion:* 59 percent of mainstreamers believe it is permissible; Hollywood, 97 percent.

- *No religious affiliation:* 4 percent of the mainstream; 45 percent of the TV crowd.[1]

More and more, research is telling us that television does indeed mold the behaviors of our children. For example, children who watch at least three hours a day are far more likely to commit acts of violence. Social scientists have concluded that there is a "numbing effect," in which something seen over and over becomes less shocking and more acceptable.[2] On the other hand, *Effective Clinical Practice* published a study demonstrating that teens whose parents restrict them from watching R-rated movies are one-third as likely to smoke or drink as kids who have no such restrictions.[3]

Is that, then, the answer? Simply restrict our children from as much of the world as possible? Does this mean unplugging our televisions, our video players, and our relationships with anyone else who dips into the murky waters of this culture?

Surely there must be some other response that is less drastic. We as Christians are called to be the light of the world and the salt of the earth. That means we must somehow be integrated into this culture, representing a spiritual alternative to the darkness that surrounds us. And we know that through the power of Christ and in the guidance of the Holy Spirit, all things are possible. Our Lord will protect us as surely as he shielded Daniel from the claws of the lions.

Just the same, these are our precious children. We want them to grow up to be wise, mature young men and women of integrity. How can we deal wisely and effectively with a rampaging Media Monster? Again, the answer can be found in one word: training. We cannot fully regulate every bit of sensory information that our children will encounter through their teenage years. What we *can* do is teach and train, so that our children can discern for themselves what to treasure—and what to trash.

A VAST WASTELAND

Listen to the words of a prominent critic:

> I invite you to sit down in front of your television set when your station goes on the air and stay there without a book, magazine, newspaper, profit-and-loss sheet or rating book to distract you—and keep your eyes glued to that set until the station signs off. I can assure you that you will observe a vast wasteland.
>
> You will see a procession of game shows, violence, audience-participation shows, formula comedies about totally unbelievable families, blood and thunder, mayhem, violence, sadism, murder, western bad men, western good men, private eyes, gangsters, more violence and cartoons. And, endlessly, commercials—many screaming, cajoling and offending.[4]

Would you be surprised to learn that these words were spoken nearly forty-five years ago? Newton Minow's classic speech coined the phrase "vast wasteland" to refer to our television terrain. And his words are truer than ever—in fact, most parents would be thrilled to return to the kind of content television carried in 1961. Sex, violence, and rampant greed are far less controlled than they were in the days of the Television Code, an official guideline that read,

Television and all who participate in it are jointly accountable to the American public for respect for the special needs
of children, for community responsibility, for the advance-
ment of education and culture, for the acceptability of the
program materials chosen, for decency and decorum in
production, and for propriety in advertising.[5]

The cultural arsenal is far more sophisticated and diversi-
fied today, and far more reckless. Those who look out for the
welfare of children are like voices crying in the wilderness.
Television is only the beginning. We need to think in terms of
several other media sources.

The Internet

We have reached a time when fewer households are supervised
by a parent in the home after school. Children are little information factories, and they thrive on the hypertextual wonder-
land of cyberspace. It's colorful, it's interactive, and it's
engrossing. Many children's television shows and commercials
direct children to their Web sites, offering tantalizing incen-
tives to check the Web page and to register, providing valuable
information to some corporation.

Since children love to experiment, they will type in various
site names (URLs) to see what is there. And if your daughter
types in something like "www.girls.com" or the like, she may
well come across a pornography site. She'll instantly see images
that no child should encounter.

The chat-room phenomenon, too, has been well-docu-
mented. Chat rooms are "instant-message" boards where
Internet users type messages to one another in small groups in

real time. But many pedophiles have been rooted out of some of these chat rooms, where they posed as children and—in some cases—attempted to make an appointment for contact with the child.

For these and many other reasons, you have an obvious mandate to very closely supervise your child's Internet activity—if any. Many parents are putting computers in their children's rooms for the convenience of homework or games. But you should think twice about this idea. It makes good sense to keep the computer in a public place—the kitchen, playroom, or family room, for example—where it's easier to supervise your child's activity.

You should also be strict in setting limits on amount of usage. As television was the great addiction in past years, now it is the Internet that is getting its hooks into our children's time.

It's a wonderful idea to look into family-friendly Internet filtering software. Frankly, many adults are slow to adopt these programs because they can present some inconveniences. They may inadvertently block very appropriate sites the adults wish to visit, for example. But whatever may be the trade-offs, you can be far more effective in preventing certain words or subjects from darkening your home with a good filtering program. There are a number of options. To find the best and most timely for your family, simply do a bit of wise comparison shopping. Type the words *family, filtering,* and *software* into the window of a search engine such as Google or Yahoo, and look carefully for a site that compares and contrasts various programs.

Let me also say here and now that we as parents need to do a much better job of keeping up with emerging technology. Our older children are certainly doing that, and we can't be effective stewards of our households if we don't understand how things work. We hear of many parents who are relying on their kids to set up their computers, program their VCRs, and so forth. You need not become a techno-guru to simply understand the basics of programs and their set-up.

As we'll see below, one of the primary reasons the V-chip failed was that parents were uncertain how it worked and how to use it. Such tools as Internet filters can be very useful, but they're useless if we allow our children to become the electronic gatekeepers of our households.

TV, the V-Chip, and Viewer Ratings

In the year 2000, Congress mandated that all televisions would include the V-chip (*V* for violence) as a response to the worsening trends in television programming. But this program is widely regarded as a failure.

> The Annenberg Center recently studied households given active V-chip tech support. One hundred and ten families with children were given new TV sets containing V-chips, and most parents received extensive operating instructions. At the end of one year, 77 families reported that they'd never tried the device, while just 8 percent claimed to be using it. This percentage is likely to be higher than that for usage among the general population, who've never received any training. For the most part, it seems that parents simply don't use V-chips.[6]

The problem, then, is *not* that we can't stop the content from coming into our homes (including by using the channel remote or the off switch). The problem for many parents is that they're not willing to take the time or trouble.

The same is true with the new TV ratings. The television industry has instituted TV Parental Guideline ratings to help parents make informed viewing decisions. They're a bit more specific than the rating system we use for movies. The rating is flashed at the beginning of a show, and they include one of the following ratings plus brief specifics as to content (language, situations, and so on):

TV-Y shows are judged appropriate for all children; *TV-Y7* shows are for ages seven and above; *TV7FV* shows include "fantasy violence"; *TV-G* signifies a show not made specifically for children but thought to be safe for their viewing. *TV-PG* calls for parental guidance—and watch for the specific situations and language included beneath the rating. *TV-14* means "parents strongly cautioned," and fourteen is the industry's suggested minimum appropriate age. Finally, *TV-MA* shows are for "mature audiences only."

Keep in mind that you need not regulate your family's television viewing based on what the issuers of these ratings find appropriate. You can simply use them as a guideline to make your own informed decisions. For example, if you see the rating TV-Y7, you may decide your eight-year-old doesn't need to watch this presentation.

Also, use the Internet and other resources to find out as much information about a show as possible. Once your child has become engrossed in the story line of some movie, it causes frustration to abruptly switch the channel when something offensive crops up. Be intentional about making the right decision before the show begins.

Video Games

Some of the most distressing cultural content plays out on the screens of today's video games. These are sold for the computer as well as specialized consoles (PlayStation, Xbox, Game Boy). Again, watch the ratings; read reviews. Many of these games (particularly for teenagers) place children in the role of serial killers, soldiers, or other aggressors. As a matter of fact, spokesmen for the armed forces have commented that some of these games train the young users in the mind-set of killing; they've commissioned the game manufacturers to help them design game versions for military training.

Games such as "Grand Theft Auto" nurture a mindlessly violent, anarchic attitude toward the world. There is also a considerable degree of occult and pagan spiritualism because, of course, the manufacturers know that whatever is rebellious and forbidden proves irresistible to the adolescent mind.

Let your child know that it's important for you to preview the games he or she wants. Read the ratings carefully, and make it a habit to talk with your children about the content of games, movies, shows, music, and the rest. Help them learn to think with values-based discernment.

Hollywood and the Sex Obsession

Just as video games preach the gospel of violence, the motion-picture industry carries the constant message that life is all about sexuality and about selfish indulgence of every impulse. Think of the difference in this new world, compared to the world of past generations. Movies were governed by decency codes that forbade them to deal with sexuality any closer than the vaguest inference. When Rhett Butler uttered the final words of *Gone with the Wind* in 1939—"I don't give a damn"—there was swirling controversy and widespread disapproval.

Now consider the films that surround our children. It's not that there are no more wholesome movies for children—there are actually more of them than ever. The problem is that there are so many unsuitable titles that lure children and adolescents. And the local multiplex is harder for us to guard than our own television sets. Ratings are supposed to govern who can get into a PG-13 or R-rated film, but enforcement is uniformly lax.

At the right time, we need to train our children to have a healthy and balanced view of sexuality. And we need to help them see the emptiness of what the world is selling them. Specifically, we need to model faithful, biblical marriage and the rewards of "just saying no" and waiting for marriage. We need to talk about the sin that is committed against women (or men) when they are approached as sex objects.

Is this really a serious problem? Isn't it true that "everyone" goes to these movies or reads these magazines in the new world? I wish you could talk to Frank, a troubled young man whom I counseled several years ago. A friendly and sensible thirty-five-year-old with strong values, Frank was nonetheless troubled by many things—not the least of which were his relationships with the opposite sex. He suffered from depression and guilt.

In time, Frank shared that pornography had deeply influenced his life and his inner thoughts. His parents had never allowed such materials in the home, but a friend named Jack had shared them. In fact, Jack's mother provided lewd magazines and watched pay-per-view sex movies with the boys.

I saw the disruption to Frank's life, as well as to the lives of other young men and women I have counseled. Sex is a wonderful gift from God, set at the very foundation of the family unit that he created. That's why the distortion and exploitation of sexuality are capable of crumbling the foundations of an entire society. Surely we can see the truth of that as we look around the cityscape of today in this bleak new world.

Parents often point out that it's difficult to know what their children are seeing at the mall multiplex. If they're untrustworthy, they could claim to be on their way to a PG movie, then substitute one with a more adult rating. Your goal, of course, is to reach a point when your teenager has honesty and integrity and can be trusted when out of your sight. But if you're not certain what film your child has attended, plan on asking some simple questions the next day. Read reviews of the films in question, and make sure your child attended the appropriate film.

If King David, a man after God's own heart, could nearly see his kingdom destroyed after giving in to sexual temptation, how much more vigilant must we be to keep our homes and our children clean? Broken and contrite, David prayed, "Create in me a pure heart, O God, and renew a steadfast spirit within me" (Psalm 51:10). We might adapt that to read, "Create for us a pure home, O God, and renew a steadfast spirit within its walls."

FIGHTING FIRE WITH FIRE

All is not lost. When the darkness falls, the light of the candle is far more powerful. You and your family will live amid an unrelenting barrage of messages and media that range from unpleasant to unacceptable. Yet image after image presents you with an opportunity to teach and to train.

You can keep the worst of it out of your home through vigilant stewardship of the "gates" by which these things enter. You can use Internet filtering, television supervision, and guidelines about which movies can be seen. But far more effective will be the gradual process of shaping the young minds in your home. Talk about what you see and hear. Encourage your kids to take a good look at song lyrics, and ask them, "What are these singers and songwriters trying to teach you? How do you feel about them trying to teach you those kinds of values?" Point to the underlying messages in movies and TV shows, Web sites and video games. Ask questions like: "Do you believe we should select friends or mates based merely on physical appearance? Do you believe celebrities are really more special or important than ordinary individuals, as this show implies?"

Teach the right values early, then reinforce them by using all that you see and hear as a family. If you instruct gently, consistently, and effectively, your children will come to the conclusions you want them to have, and they will learn to protect themselves. After all, you won't always be around to serve as a filter; after a certain age, your child will resent your more aggressive protectionism anyway, and you can create a backlash of stealth anger.

The apostle Paul reminds us not to forget the actual *candle*. That's the lovely light that chases out darkness. He wrote, "Whatever is true, whatever is noble, whatever is right, whatever is pure, whatever is lovely, whatever is admirable—if anything is excellent or praiseworthy—think about such things" (Philippians 4:8). How can you apply this principle? You can be proactive in guiding your children not away from

culture entirely but toward good and deserving art and litera-
ture. Teach your children that verse and show them how to use
it to help with discernment. Which selection has nobility,
purity, loveliness, excellence, and praiseworthiness: the new
teenage slasher movie, or *Ben-Hur*?

As you point to such decisions, keep things as positive as
possible. We certainly don't want to further the sad notion that
our faith is all about prohibitions and "thou shalt not's." Make
your home a culturally safe haven, but make it a fun place, too,
filled with enjoyable activities and particularly love and
laughter. Until a couple of generations ago, no family in
human history needed a television set. You can prove that
family life is more enjoyable and memorable when you keep
viewing to the minimum in your household.

Our son David attended his high-school reunion and filled
out a questionnaire concerning memories of the adolescent
days. For the favorite hangout, his former classmates rated our
home second after a local restaurant. David's friends didn't see
our home as a dull and strait-laced place with puritanical
values; they saw it as a fun hangout. And the best part of it was
that while our children's friends were enjoying our home, we
were getting to know them, too. Some of them still stay in
touch.

Your mission is to help your children think and behave
Christianly in an unchristian world. Then they can not only
protect themselves against the worst spiritual assaults, but they
can ultimately do something about it. Perhaps your son will go
to Hollywood someday and produce excellent, noble, and
praiseworthy cinema. Perhaps your daughter will be a singer of
good and worthy lyrics and a role model whom tomorrow's
parents can feel good about.

TV VIEWING GUIDELINES

Finally, here are some simple and practical guidelines for using the television in your home:

- Definitely use time limits. Many children will watch the television for as many hours as they're allowed. My recommendation is between sixty and ninety minutes a day.

- Use a TV viewing guide and select what shows and channels are permissible.

- Allow your child to choose from the range you make available.

- Enforce "No-Tube Zones": before school, when it slows everyone down; after school, until homework is done; and during any family meal.

- Be firm about your schedule, approved shows, and time limits. Exceptions create precedent.

- Never use television as a cheap baby-sitter.

- Encourage alternatives—from toys in the beginning, to reading, music, and the outdoors.

- Keep good tapes and DVDs around for family entertainment and interaction.

- When your children do watch, join them if at all possible. Then talk about what you've seen.

- Always understand the various kinds of technology at use in your home.

A closing word of encouragement: Don't be overwhelmed; don't panic. Always remember that the weapons in the arsenal of the Christian—truth, righteousness, the Word of God, and his Spirit—are always more powerful than anything with which the world can confront us. There is no silly movie, no superficial television show, no passing song that can hope to compete with the power of the loving community within your family. When you're relating well together, communicating effectively, controlling anger, and dealing with each of life's new stages joyfully, your children will follow your lead. Just as they trust you to guide them to safe play and safe food, they will trust your wisdom in these other things.

Remember Paul's list of the fruit of spiritual living? These fruit apply to the spiritual family as well, and they include "love, joy, peace, patience, kindness, goodness, faithfulness, gentleness and self-control. *Against such things there is no law*" (Galatians 5:22–23, emphasis added). Note my emphasis on those final words. They are telling you that no laws or restrictions or value systems can match the power of love, joy, peace, and the rest. These make up the wonderful light that emanates from the candle that lights your family's way through the darkness. As you hold that light high, your children will draw near to you. Trust them to choose your light over the world's darkness.

7 NURTURING YOUNG SPIRITS

Do you ever look at your children, squint your eyes a bit, and visualize how they'll turn out as adults?

I imagine every parent has done that at one time or another. We can see pictures of adults when they were children, but the only picture of our children as adults is the conception we keep in our imaginations. We think of the mature, wise, and well-adjusted young adults we want them to become. We imagine them selecting a pleasing spouse who will add joy and newness to our extended family. We can picture ourselves in our older years, sitting by the Christmas tree and surrounded by laughing, grown children with, of course, the noise and commotion of our grandchildren. What a great way to begin the golden years of our lives: beaming with pride as our children go out into the world happy, successful, and fruitful in the world at large and in the kingdom of God.

Speaking personally, I could not have imagined a happier moment than one I cherish from recent years. There were my wife, Pat, and I, sitting on the front row in church, watching our younger son, Dale, taking Kisha as his wife. Few moments can top that, surrounded in God's house by precious family and intimate friends, sharing a moment of moments—the culmination of all our past parenting and all our future hopes. In instances such as these, we feel time intersect with eternity.

I sat with Pat's hand in mine, thanking God silently and profoundly for the magnificent scope of his blessings on our family. In my mind's eye I could see Dale again, a child learning to speak, to walk, to obey. I thought of the games we had played together, the arguments we had endured, the momentous discussions we had shared. So much of me, so much of my wife, poured into this young adult—and hopefully so much of God, too. Now came the harvesttime: Dale beginning his own family with a genuine, beautiful young Christian woman. I prayed, *Father, how could I ever begin to thank you enough?*

And I knew that as full as my joy was at that moment, surely the joy of our Father was even deeper and wider. I thrive on the happiness of my children, and my heavenly Father thrives on my happiness. He thrives on yours, too. He wants your life to culminate in many moments like this when you see that, yes, all the blood, sweat, and tears of parenting really brought these tender young shoots to blossom.

And to reach that goal, we cannot fail to transmit to our children the most important truths of all. We need to show them the reality of our faith and lead them toward that one thing they must do for themselves: make it their own. We can read them Bible stories, pray with them at bedtime, and raise them in the loving environment of a church. But that rite of passage must come when they reach out with the sixth sense of faith and encounter God for themselves.

Otherwise, can we really feel we have succeeded as parents? Jesus said, "What good is it for a man to gain the whole world, yet forfeit his soul?" (Mark 8:36). The wisdom of that truth is being lost on many parents today, who are spending more time training their children (either intentionally or unintentionally) to "gain the whole world" than to seek the treasures that will satisfy the soul.

We see so many young people dropping out of church, and we wonder, What can I do to keep this from happening to my kids? One researcher spent years studying devout young Christians and came to the conclusion that most of them were the product of either a home where the parents loved and followed Christ seriously or a dramatic teenage conversion due to a powerful youth ministry. The great gap, he concluded, came in the homes of churchgoers who lacked genuine passion for their faith.[1]

Your faith, then, is likely to be caught in whatever genuine form you possess it. If you love the Lord deeply, your children are likely to follow your lead—providing, of course, that they feel well loved by you. If that doesn't happen, then faith will become one more battlefield between you, and perhaps one of the most significant.

WHERE SPIRITUAL TRAINING BEGINS

Once again, then, we come to the very foundation thought of this book: Provide your children with unconditional love and acceptance. Do that, and they are likely to embrace your faith along with many other wonderful things you will share.

Faith and feelings overlap; they are not separate entities but are closely connected. Love lays the foundation for spiritual faith, and faith sharing enhances our love within the family. Therefore you should realize that from the moment of your child's birth, you are working toward her spiritual formation simply by providing love, warmth, and security. No other factor is more important.

Next comes the role of experience. Every human being carries the complexity of the cosmos—did you know that? There are more than one hundred billion neurons in the mind of your child, as many as stars that shine in the Milky Way. Over the course of life and growth, these neurons will gradually become connected and operational. Experience—much of which is under your control in the beginning—defines the result of all this neural development. Genetic factors, of course, play a great part as well. Your child is born with a rough molecular blueprint of the many functions life will require. During that first year, there is inconceivably tremendous development in the "neuron highways" that are paved throughout the brain of your child. Then, by age ten, the lesser or unused neural highways and back roads are shut down. What remains is a unique human being, an individual like no other who lives or who has ever lived—a child with a distinct soul.

If the environment hasn't been stimulating during the first three years, if there hasn't been play, if there hasn't been physical touch and interaction of various kinds, and if there has been any lack of basic care or nourishment, then this child will have a brain 20 to 30 percent smaller than normal.

Your child, then, is not a blank slate; neither is she a fully programmed genetic complex preset to function in various ways. The consensus of neurobiologists is that the child is a human creature awaiting the treatment and experiences that will mold and shape his personality. The brain immediately goes to work developing the full range of emotions required by the human experience. The newborn basically feels distress or contentment and little in between, but from the age of two months, we see the emergence of joy and sadness, envy and empathy, pride and resentment.

Unpleasant as it may be, think about a child who is physically abused in early childhood. This little one will fine-tune the range of emotions that comes with danger and fear. Those circuits will be among the first and most powerful to connect within that small brain. If the abuse comes early, the damage can be devastating.

I pray you have not been so unfortunate as to be a product of such experiences, yet the broad principle is worth consideration. Do you ever experience emotions that surprise you, feelings you can't really explain? You have been "wired" early on in life in ways that still bring about certain emotional reactions.

Reflect, then, on the child surrounded by joy, warmth, laughter, and music. The foundation blocks are there for your child to be all you could hope or wish. These first months and years are so important.

Early Adolescence

Onward to the age of ten, then, your child is developing mentally at a rapid rate—laying those "information highways" in every direction inside his hungry, developing mind. And about that time, the unused information routes are closed down, while the brain expands the active neural paths into "superhighways."

For many years, scientists believed that the adolescent brain was a fully formed mind—that, by puberty, all the construction work was complete. It was always my observation, however, that teenagers are closer to children in their thinking than to adults. We now know that those neural circuits are still being established into the early twenties.

This is a very crucial issue. All the potential that your child has can be nurtured or squandered during this time, based on the way you train and guide your child. As the parent, you are the one encouraging some patterns of feelings and emotion while discouraging others. The very best parenting needs to be done during these early years: teaching obedience, encouraging creativity, rewarding cooperation, and so on. At the same time, negative patterns can be all but closed down. How resilient will your child be? How will she cope with stress? Will her general outlook be positive or negative, eager or fearful? What kind of self-concept will she have—will she see herself as a gifted, capable, and well-loved child of God and of her parents, or something far short of that? Every morning, every day, every afternoon and evening with your child, you are reinforcing or discouraging certain channels that will set in for life.

These recent landmark scientific studies have shown us more than ever that the positive, proactive parent can have a remarkable effect on the life of a child. Yes, there are genetically predetermined factors, but God has given you a wide range for helping your child become a masterpiece.

Building the Foundation

By the teen years, then, the networks of neural patterns—the information highways—are laid down. Adolescence is all about learning to manage all those behaviors in a more mature and responsible way. We know that even as kids begin to look more to their wider relational circle of peers, it is still the parents who are the primary influence. Teenagers recognize that their faith, their morals, and their values have been guided and shaped by their adult mentors in the home.

As a cautionary example of what can go wrong, we endured the psychodrama of the presidential impeachment hearings several years ago. I watched a Barbara Walters interview with Monica Lewinsky, whose extramarital affair with the president brought so much shame to the nation and to the White House. As she answered the interview questions, Ms. Lewinsky gave a picture of a very confused young lady—a serial adulterer whose motives, goals, and self-concept seemed to bring self-destruction again and again. With all the furor this event created, she seemed to possess no regard for the consequences of her actions or for the damage she had helped inflict on her country and its leadership.

As a parent, seeing your child turn out in that moral territory would amount to a personal nightmare. Yet there are more positive models all around us—young men and women who honor their upbringing by their actions, their demeanor, and the difference they make in the world. These young adults have come of age in the same moral environment as the poor role models we see, but they have been provided by their parents with a powerful, enduring foundation of character and values.

In the Old Testament, we read the story of the Israelites founding a new country and a new society. As they crossed the Jordan River into Canaan, God established for them the foundation by which the people should morally train their children:

Love the LORD your God with all your heart and with all your soul and with all your strength. These commandments that I give you today are to be upon your hearts. Impress them on your children. Talk about them when you sit at home and when you walk along the road, when you lie down and when you get up. Tie them as symbols on your hands and bind them on your foreheads. Write them on the doorframes of your houses and on your gates. (Deuteronomy 6:5–9)

The first and most important line of that, of course, is familiar. And we need to remember that Jesus added a corollary that he said was "like it": "Love your neighbor as yourself" (Matthew 22:39). We want our children to understand this foundation for all that we do in this life: to love God and to love others. In the Deuteronomy passage, we see the emphasis of using every experience as a teaching opportunity. Everything in and around the home should be built around the training we are providing for our children.

Notice that the overwhelming message here is that, yes, you should share your faith with your children. I have observed parents from the "let them make up their own minds" school. They somehow feel that all human beings should adopt or reject faith in a vacuum, carefully selecting from various options with no influence from the parents. This kind of "politically correct" thinking deprives the child of the shared faith experience she craves. Not teaching is just another way of teaching—teaching faithlessness, in this case. In any event, those who are truly devoted to their Lord cannot hide it. It's absurd to think they could raise their children without some of that faith experience soaking in.

SHARING GOD

We do want to pass on our beliefs. We want to share ideas and principles, values and goals. But in the end, we will have failed if we do not share the Lord himself, in all his vitality and power. God is personal, and we experience him within ourselves—and yet he can be shared. He longs to be shared.

Let your children see more than just your ideas *about* God. Your children will look on you like the Gentiles who approached Philip the disciple and said, "Sir, . . . we would like to see Jesus" (John 12:21). They had heard enough about him to want to hear *from* him. Can you doubt your children's eagerness to experience the reality of God by your side? Include them in prayer times. Encourage them to ask God to bless them in a special way the next day, then to watch and see how God does so. Children are capable of enjoying significant relationships with their Lord.

As a matter of fact, they are our model. Jesus said that *we* are the ones who need to be more like them in the way we approach God, not the other way around (Matthew 18:3–4). We are all God's *children,* not God's "grownups." This fact creates a wonderful common ground for you and your children: experiencing God together. You need not have all the answers to every theological question, and you need not convince your children you are some form of saint or spiritual giant. Share with them that you love God, that you are trying to know more of him, and that following him is life's greatest adventure. Share your prayer experiences, and ask them to pray for you when you have a need—they will feel respected when you do so, and they will pray sincerely for you.

In these ways you are creating a spiritual atmosphere in

your home. It is often said that children may stray from the fold as they become young adults, but if we have trained them well, they will always return. There is probably some truth to this. But if you have a wonderful, caring relationship with your children, and if you raise them in a good, vibrant church and with active, joyful spirituality in your home—why would they ever want to leave in the first place?

We often fail to realize that our teaching is more than what we verbalize. There are homes where children are absolutely drilled in doctrine so they are able to enumerate every fundamental of the faith backward and forward—but they know less of the spirit of the law than its letter. What we tell our children about God is a smaller part of the lesson than what we live—and particularly the feelings that come across. We've all seen those family cars on the way to church, filled with quarreling parents and kids. Are faith and church matters of joy in your household or matters of duty? What emotions would your children associate with God?

If you were to teach them only one lesson about God, I believe it should be that God is Love. "We know and rely on the love God has for us. God is love. Whoever lives in love lives in God, and God in him" (1 John 4:16). The two essentials in your home are your own relationship with God and the unconditional love that ultimately unites you, your children, and the Lord. Many parents use God as a guilt tool ("God knows if you're lying right now! God saw you steal that cookie!"). They don't realize they're saddling their children with a lifelong image of God as an avenging heavenly sheriff. It's no wonder that many young adults flee from such a God and that many of them—even in counseling—must struggle for years to free themselves of such concepts.

Instead, we want God to be associated with smiles, music, and laughter in our homes. We want our children to grasp the idea that his unconditional love and mercy are absolute—that he loves our kids just as we do. We want to remind them that even before they were born, he knew them and looked forward to the wonderful surprises he has for their lives. And it helps to use examples from our own lives, past and present. How did God bring you and your spouse together? How did you come to know him better during a tough time? What blessings has he showered on your life? These are emotional experiences, and your children will connect with them and therefore connect with God.

You'll make wonderful memories this way. I think immediately of a fishing trip in North Carolina with my two sons. We were having so much fun that we couldn't stop fishing once darkness had fallen. As we sat out by the water, we saw the moon and the stars come out. What a clear night it was—even the Milky Way was clear and awesome. Quite naturally we began to discuss the wonder of creation. "The heavens declare the glory of God; the skies proclaim the work of his hands" (Psalm 19:1).

Dave, my older son, commented on how small he felt there beneath the blue canopy. I told him that, yes, God's creation is immense, but he cares about every small detail of our lives. He knows the number of hairs on our heads. And no matter how small we may be, he loves us far more than stars or planets. I said, "I'm thankful that one so powerful is also so good."

"Why is he good, Dad?" asked Dale.

"I don't know," I replied. "There is so much I'm not capable of understanding about him, but I understand how much he loves me. I know it because I feel his love every day, and because he has given me two wonderful gifts in my sons, with whom I can enjoy this starry sky. And I know that even as we enjoy him right now, he is enjoying and loving us."

Those are teachable moments that can make a significant impact in the lives of your children and your family. Faith is caught before it is effectively taught. This happens when the teaching is overwhelmingly positive. Using the negative has the reverse effect.

TOOLS FOR TEACHING

In your family, life is the canvas for the great picture you are painting. It is a picture of what a successful life looks like in every regard. Your children are learning from you how to think, how to deal with feelings, how to interrelate with others, how to think about God and faith issues, how to approach responsibilities, and all the rest. Your child sees how you do these things; he splashes a few of his own colors on the canvas experimentally. As he grows, you will paint a beautiful picture together.

Here are some of your tools for teaching:

Stories and Events

Life is one great story broken up into many smaller ones. There are stories that occur on the playground, stories that occur at the beach during a family vacation, stories from the office and the church. All around are incidents, accidents, precedents. Use these stories as Jesus used his parables to show what works and what doesn't work in life. You need not be overly pedantic and take the fun out of everything with an object lesson—just make certain your children become adept at isolating the underlying values and moral lessons that are implied in every single human event. As we've seen, television shows, songs, and movies make good teaching ground because they have already engaged the attention of your children.

It's one thing to tell your children the story of Noah and how he labored on that ark even as his friends ridiculed him and went about their self-destructive lives. But your children will learn that same lesson better, for example, at the food court in your local mall, when you point out how a particular restaurant chain remains closed on Sunday to honor the Sabbath, even though more money could be made.

Your Own Experiences

Children are fascinated by the idea of their parents as children. It's hard for them to believe such a reality could ever have taken place. They like hearing about what life was like when you grew up, when people listened to phonograph records and had only three channels on the television. Tell them how you first encountered God. Tell them what happened when you did something you knew was wrong. Talk about your own life lessons.

Most of all, however, emphasize the present tense rather than the past. As you're making a difficult decision with your career, let your children participate in the moment. Encourage them to pray with you. Show them how you have laid out the options, the pros and the cons, and how you are deciding. The lessons they will learn from the reality of the situation will be profound. And as they pray with you, they will see that God is *real*—he is involved in real-life situations and is more than someone encountered in Bible stories.

Modeling Forgiveness

If you want to specialize in one particular lesson, this is a good one to select. So many people today struggle to forgive. As Philip Yancey points out in his book *What's So Amazing About Grace?* forgiveness is the most difficult and radical action we can undertake—because it is not fair! When we practice grace, we refuse to take an eye for an eye. We give love where it may not even be deserved. Nothing will teach your children more about the powerful reality of God than the experience of true forgiveness. On the other hand, what does it say about your faith if they know you have never forgiven your own parents or a sibling or an old business partner? Throughout their lives, your children will find themselves in situations where they can either take on a new burden of unresolved anger and bitterness or grow in the cleansing act of grace. Live out a beautiful lesson of mercy and forgiveness in your home.

OPTIMISM AND HOPE

Can you think of anything we need more in this new world than optimism and hope? This is a cynical world. Our art is decadent. Our political parties have become more vicious and negative than ever. Our culture teaches empty nihilism and hopelessness and attempts to make it somehow "sexy." When your teenage children encounter the voices of gloom and doom telling them this is the final generation, the world is ruined, and life is pointless—help them challenge the fallacy of that viewpoint. Our lives and our futures are in the hands of God, and he is always trustworthy.

Dr. Jerome Groopman of Harvard Medical School worked with patients with serious diseases and came to the conclusion that hope is as important for the suffering as anything he could prescribe medically. He stated, "I think hope has been, is, and always will be the heart of medicine and healing." We "could not live without hope." And even with all the medical technology available to us now, he said, "we still come back to this profound human need to believe that there is a possibility to reach a future that is better than the one in the present."[2]

This whole world can be seen as a clinic filled with suffering people. Be certain that your household is a sanctuary of hope, a place where there is always a can-do attitude. Don't catch that cultural virus of cynicism. Teach your children beautiful verses such as this one: "'I know the plans I have for you,' declares the LORD, 'plans to prosper you and not to harm you, plans to give you hope and a future'" (Jeremiah 29:11). And "Do not fear, for I am with you; do not be dismayed, for I am your God. I will strengthen you and help you; I will uphold you with my righteous right hand" (Isaiah 41:10).

You want your children to have the following truth engraved in their minds: God makes us two promises about the hard times of this life—he will go with us, and he will give us strength. This two-pronged promise is repeated throughout the Bible.

There are times when we are afraid, but we can do almost anything if someone promises to go with us and help us. God makes that very promise to your children. The world is dark and menacing, but your home is a sanctuary where your children can and should learn to find spiritual strength to sustain them. Use any and every opportunity to help them draw nearer to the God who will continue to father them even after their earthly parents have left this earth.

8 COPING WITH FEAR, ANXIETY, AND DEPRESSION

O N SEPTEMBER 11, 2001, America and its families were transformed forever within two unthinkable hours.

All in one morning, the world seemed to become a different place. In schools across our country, teachers struggled to find the words to tell their students that something terrible had transpired. How can one explain an act of mass terrorism to a child?

When the little ones arrived home in their buses and carpools, parents wondered whether to let them see the gruesome footage of passenger airplanes colliding with skyscrapers and workers diving from windows. Was it even possible to shield them from it?

Suddenly airports, shopping malls, stadiums, schools, and public places of all kinds were no longer ordinary slices of daily American life; they were settings where supreme care and vigilance were matters of life and death. No one could really say where or whether a terrorist might strike next. Even such an activity as walking to the mailbox took on grim overtones in the light of reports of anthrax poisoning.

America has moved on, as much as can be expected, but our world remains a frightening one for parents and children alike. The reality is that international tensions and technology have combined to create a world where fear is actually a commonsense necessity. We would be foolish to ignore the dangers around us, and that's why you and I take so many more precautions than our parents and grandparents before us. We no longer leave our homes unlocked at night. We have sophisticated alarm systems even on our automobiles, and we never let our younger children out of our sight.

As human beings, we are adaptable—at least those of us who are adults. We cope with the new realities and find ways to keep life going, for our jobs and our families. But we need to realize that children are sensitive. They pick up on so many fears and dangers that surround us. These days, children are routinely warned at an early age to "never talk to strangers." We keep them closer to home during their playtimes than we were kept. Every autumn, the old traditional trick or treat is largely confined to churches, malls, and safe havens, because we fear that some predator may tamper with the candy. There is no doubt that these, the most modern and "civilized" of all times, are also the most frightening days to be alive.

Parents face at least four basic fears:

1. Fear for our children in the dangers they face

2. Fear of our children's behavior and the uncertainty of discipline

3. Fear of the child himself

4. Fear of teenagers in general

FEAR FOR OUR CHILDREN

Parents today worry about the limits of their protection. How can they shield their children from a world so filled with ugliness and actual danger?

Younger parents are actually afraid of parenting—some are reluctant to build families as a result. "Will I make a good parent? Can a little child count on me?" They need to know that God will equip them, just as he has equipped parents since the beginning of time. They also need to partner with "veteran" parents who know the ropes. Look for more mature and experienced couples you know who have done an outstanding job in their own households. Buy them a cup of coffee and ask for advice. Find out what has worked for them. Even beyond the practical tips, the voice of experience will reassure you.

It's not always a bad thing to be afraid. It makes sense to have a healthy respect for the demands of parenting—it's better to approach it with a few trepidations than a load of carelessness. Though you will be learning on the job, you also want to get it right the first time without making damaging mistakes. In a culture such as ours, there won't be many second chances.

FEAR OF OUR CHILDREN'S BEHAVIOR

Some parents are afraid their children will have a tantrum or will rebel in some unpleasant way. Therefore they go too easy, letting their children gain control of the household. We see far too many homes today where the children seem to be calling the shots and the parents are actually buckling under the tyranny of their children's behavior. Once this pattern is in place, the child will push it further and further, past the limit. He will see just how much control he can have. Therefore, we have the permissive home that has become so common today.

Again, the child's emotional tank may be empty. The true subtext of the misbehavior may be, "Do you love me?" The child waits to see if the parent will take loving but corrective action. It's very difficult to deal with a child who feels unloved—nothing seems to work. Reactive punishment only makes things worse. The child becomes angry and resentful, and even more defiant. It's a vicious cycle that opens the door for children to manipulate their parents' actions. Ultimately Mom and Dad throw up their hands in despair and say, "Just give him what he wants. Do whatever will make him pipe down." And this is a terrible mistake.

The other extreme, of course, is rigid authoritarianism. The parents react with force and fearsomeness. Stern discipline, they think, will control the behavior. But what about that child with the empty tank? Will the increasingly strict punishment make that child feel loved? Of course not. The punishment trap is a breeding place for anger and ultimately "stealth anger" that emerges in irrational behavior.

Children don't need to detect our fear of them—they need to detect our love for them. Therefore, we must not resort to either the paralysis that leads to permissiveness or the rigidity that leads to rage. These are both extremes that are bound to fail. Look around you, and you will see examples in homes everywhere. Instead, as we've seen through this book, we must begin with unconditional love and build a relational parenting model from there.

FEAR OF THE CHILD HIMSELF

Arising from our fear of the child's behavior is a fear of the child himself. When behavior becomes a huge issue, we don't know what to expect. Particularly as children become teenagers, they can actually become menacing to their parents. Any child will sense this fear and take advantage of it. Again, fear takes control of the relationship, and effective parenting becomes impossible. At all times, parents must be firmly but lovingly in control of their households. The moment children begin to run things, the family has a great problem on its hands.

FEAR OF TEENAGERS IN GENERAL

It's really an old, old story: Kids dress differently, carry themselves differently, cluster in groups, and just seem to have some look on their faces that makes us uncertain. Today, there are tattoos and facial jewelry and low-slung pants. But in past generations it was other things. Some people assume any group of laughing adolescents is looking for some kind of trouble, but the truth is that kids today are made of the same basic human fiber as kids of all generations. They are still created in God's image, no matter what fashion accessories they choose, and they have good hearts that need love and acceptance desperately. What is different is that fewer of them are receiving that love. More of them are seeing their parents' marriages break down. More of them are reacting to the many uncertainties of a frightening world. But pay some attention to the kids in the youth group at your church or at the high school down the street, and you'll quickly be attracted to their humor, their energy, and their sincerity. These kids are getting involved in mission and service projects in unprecedented numbers. Just as there are frightening signs, there are just as many encouraging ones.

These are good young people—just as there have always been. They want to know you better. They want this to be a strong and healthy world. More than anything, they want to find a place to fit in and to be loved. Yes, we know all about the extremes of drug abuse, sexual illicitness, and criminal behavior. Our job is to provide enough love and caring that fewer teenagers will drift in that direction. We need to overcome our fear of them, reject the media stereotypes of young thugs (partly to blame for our fears), and build relational bridges to these young, energetic, and multitalented young people. They are creating the world that our own children will one day inhabit.

BEYOND OUR FEARS

Here is a fact: Your child is going to grow up. There are times when watching her grow is bittersweet. We wish we could slow down—just for a while. We like our children at age three, but then we find that we like them at age four in a different way, then at age five and age six as well. We might miss the fun of having a toddler. But the fact is that each age and stage brings fresh new delights. Once we reach that point when we can read aloud to our children, we would never want to revert to some earlier stage. Once we reach the time when we can converse intelligently with them, we like this new stage better than we thought.

It's a shame that so many of our older friends roll their eyes and cynically tell us, "Enjoy it now—just wait until they're teenagers." Our world conditions us to resist that particular crucial time frame, and some parents actually try to delay the normal rites of passage that go with adolescence. Please realize that your child is God's workmanship (Ephesians 2:10), lovingly crafted by God to blossom in some new and wonderful way at every juncture. Don't fear, but *enjoy*. If you follow the simple and healthy goals of unconditional love and acceptance, along with proactive, relational approaches to your child, your bond and mutual enjoyment will only grow richer, deeper, and more rewarding. Your maturing child will have more to give back for all that you have given. Therefore I tell parents that when they feel the pangs of fear and uncertainty, relax! Take a deep breath, and realize that God is with you and that there is no age or stage your child can enter that millions of parents before you have not faced and handled beautifully. Then all four of these basic fears will vaporize.

THE CHALLENGE OF ANXIETY

Mom sits up late at night, brewing coffee and waiting for her seventeen-year-old son to return from his first evening date and his first solo excursion with the family car. She trusts her son. She knows he will drive carefully and that he will arrive home at the hour he promised. So why does she feel so "wired" and unable to relax?

Anxiety is a complex behavior, fear's first cousin. It's in

many ways a good emotion with ill effects. After all, anxiety ties us in knots inside. It increases blood pressure, even causes feelings of panic in some cases. But we feel anxiety because we care about someone. Every parent knows that powerful drive to protect the child at all costs. From the moment we become parents, we are constantly on our guard.

Anxiety, then, is the protective fluid that greases the gears of parenting. If your son is outdoors, you want to know exactly where, and you give strict instructions in how far he can roam. Then, as long as he's out of your sight, you're never quite relaxed. Too little anxiety would be poor parenting (such people tend to lack compassion), but too much is unhealthy for us. Some parents spend the latter part of the evening riffling through a child's knapsack, making sure every test paper has been signed, every homework assignment has been done, and no detail has been forgotten. Naturally, such parents tend to usurp responsibility and rob their children of learning important lessons in maturity.

What we need is a balance of loving concern and trusting acceptance. It's good to remember the startlingly simple prescription of Jesus in the Sermon on the Mount:

> I tell you, do not worry about your life, what you will eat or drink; or about your body, what you will wear . . . But seek first his kingdom and his righteousness, and all these things will be given to you as well. Therefore do not worry about tomorrow, for tomorrow will worry about itself. Each day has enough trouble of its own. (Matthew 6:25, 33–34)

And as you toss and turn in bed, worrying about some issue of parenting, it helps to repeat this passage to yourself:

Do not be anxious about anything, but in everything, by prayer and petition, with thanksgiving, present your requests to God. And the peace of God, which transcends all understanding, will guard your hearts and your minds in Christ Jesus. (Philippians 4:6–7)

Remember, finally, that anxiety is contagious. If you want your child to have a balanced approach to life, it helps for you to have one. Your constant anxiety will wear off on your son or daughter. It makes all the difference to fill that emotional tank. Provide all the love your child needs and the idea that she will be accepted and cared for no matter what. That love binds you and your child, and it dissolves anxiety. A powerful thought: "There is no fear in love. But perfect love drives out fear, because fear has to do with punishment. The one who fears is not made perfect in love" (1 John 4:18).

Alternatives: The child who is not loved unconditionally will not develop the compassion that makes up positive anxiety—he will not learn to care deeply for others, for he will not have experienced that care himself. Punishment-based parenting will build a surplus of negative anxiety in him—a worrying spirit and a general mistrust of everything that life brings.

DEPRESSION AND CHILDREN

There was a time when few people associated children with the topic of depression. The major reason was probably that we failed to identify depression as a factor in most cases. Today, it's clear that depression is hitting human emotions at earlier stages. Ronald Kessler of Harvard Medical School studied eight thousand Americans ages fifteen to fifty-four. Of those now forty-five to fifty-four, only 2 percent reported symptoms of depression by their late teens. But in the age range of fifteen to twenty-four, 23 percent reported serious depression before age twenty.[1] Today we speak of childhood and adolescent depression as an almost commonplace malady.

What are the implications? It is reported that youngsters who develop depression or anxiety are three to four times more likely than their peers to have drug or alcohol abuse problems by their midtwenties. There are also connections drawn to an epidemic of suicide. Between 1950 and 1995, suicide rates for children and teens quadrupled.

Many factors feed into this phenomenon, but it's safe to say that in most cases, severe anxiety has been previously present. Depressed children are nearly always anxiety-driven. This is happening with children from every background, rich or poor, rural or urban.

There's another interesting factor: the loss of extended families. Most sociologists point to the fact that in a career-driven, mobile society, there are fewer grandparents, aunts, and uncles around to provide that extra layer of nurture and reassurance that blessed so many children of past generations. Parents, too, have suffered from the loss of proximity to their own parents and siblings for support and counsel. In place of these former human relationships, children have computers and television sets. They spend more time alone, isolated. They become individualists and therefore struggle with the many challenges in life that demand social skills.

We can make further points about depressed children:

- They tend to come from homes of either divorce or heightened tension.

- They seem to be socially less adept; they either receive or imagine rejection and are therefore shy and withdrawn.

- They suffer from poor self-image, connecting their problems to perceived personal flaws as opposed to changeable behavior.

- They experience a great deal of stress.

- They tend not to accomplish goals, such as goals for school grades, because of their shorter attention span.

What about the question of gender? There are some important considerations here. We are discovering that depression has been significantly underdiagnosed in boys. They do in fact suffer far more from depression than is often realized. Boys' depression is often undetected because they "act it out." That is, rather than manifesting the traditionally recognized (often passive) symptoms, they take action. They may pick fights; they may steal or lie or (in the case of teenage boys) drive a car at a dangerous speed. Many males who end up in detention centers and, later, prisons have strayed because of unrecognized depression.

We see depression in girls primarily after the age of eleven. Over the next four years, we are far more likely to see it arise. At eighteen, girls have twice the rate of depression that boys have. Like adult women, girls tend to dwell more on problems than males, and therefore they slide more easily into negative mindsets. As nurturers, they suffer more from worry and anxiety. And in the teenage years they find many objects for anxiety: appearance, family problems, and popularity, for example. We tend to train our girls to be caring in orientation. Again, it's a blade that cuts both ways—they have deeper sensitivities, and in turn they can suffer from them.

Identifying Depression

Depression is misunderstood and often difficult to detect. It often hides beneath its own symptoms. For example, you would be immediately alarmed about the discovery that your child was abusing drugs, and you might miss the fact that it was merely a symptom of a more complex emotional depression.

In recent years we've grown more effective in recognizing and treating depression, both medically and therapeutically. We know that it comes on very subtly, slowly, and gradually in children. It is complex in its entanglements with its own causes and effects. If your child's grades drop off in school, you might try many responses before considering the possibility of depression. You might make the mistake of focusing on the surface problem because, again, no parent wants his or her child to struggle in school. But we will attack the problem in vain unless we deal with the root cause.

But don't forget the complexity of this problem. For example, there may be neurological factors in your child's grade problems, but they may be aggravated by the depression.

We often fail to recognize depression in our children because of our own long-term sadness and irritability—and because we are more understanding and articulate than children in the realm of emotions. Your child doesn't understand what is wrong inside. And we may consult our friends, who dismiss the problems of our children with words such as, "It's just a phase. All children go through it."

Your child's world may seem balanced and ideal. He may have friends, activities, and all that he needs and wants. This doesn't mean he is safe from depression—particularly if he is a sensitive, feeling child. We ourselves need to be sensitive to the emotional worlds of our children and humble about the fact that we never know all that is going on inside them. Every human being is a complex creation, a network of physical, mental, spiritual, and emotional factors.

In this particularly negative and often distressing world, we need to keep the environment as positive and emotionally nourishing as possible. This means making certain you watch wholesome movies and shows, build some pleasant memories and relive them as often as possible, and do all that you can do to make sure your child is around the right kind of friends and peers. Even so, we need to be informed and watchful in the area of childhood depression.

Ten Symptoms to Look For

The most practical resource we can offer is a watch list of depression symptoms. If your child displays not one but *several* of these symptoms, you should consider consultation and counseling.

1. *Shortened attention span.* Please *do not* confuse depression and attention deficit disorder (ADD). But there is some crossover: Children with ADD or ADHD (attention deficit hyperactivity disorder) tend to suffer from depression. Depression, therefore, can mimic or aggravate ADD/ADHD.

2. *Decreased concentration.* A depressed child struggles to stay on task. This sets him up for the next symptom.

3. *Daydreaming.* The child will have a wandering mind and indulge in fantasies.

4. *Boredom.* As attention wanders and decreases, the child becomes less engaged in activities he previously enjoyed.

5. *Decreased energy.* Depression and distraction can drain the child's energy. Parents will blame a lack of sleep, but this is actually a symptom of depression.

6. *Misbehavior.* Professionals also often fail to identify a child's misbehavior as a symptom of depression, but it may very well be in certain cases. Depression can also aggravate misbehavior. Examples would be disruption in school, aggressive behavior toward other children, and regressive behavior such as bedwetting or baby talk.

7. *Long-term sadness.* Any child will be sad in normally sad situations, but an enduring sadness indicates depression. Strangely enough, however, this more logical symptom is the one that is often absent.

8. *Anger.* Depression stirs up anger and aggravates existing anger issues. If your child struggles with anger, consider depression to be a possible cause.

9. *Anxiety.* Again, there is a confusing overlap. Excessive anxiety can lead to depression, but depression can also cause anxiety. For people of all ages, the link is extremely strong between these two behaviors.

10. *Withdrawal.* Depressed children tend to isolate themselves rather than interact with friends.

Treatment and Managed Care

Managed care now dominates American healthcare. It has become popular for families primarily because of its cost savings. However, managed care has made it more difficult for parents to have a child evaluated for psychological problems. Even in the face of known and serious mental illness, it is extremely difficult to get enough cooperation from an insurance company to pay for even a psychological or psychiatric evaluation. But proceeding to treatment before such an evaluation is like asking a surgeon to operate without first obtaining x-rays. The result has been an overuse or wrong use of medications.

Formerly, pediatricians were able to have a child evaluated to ascertain if the child truly suffered from attention deficit hyperactivity disorder and if a psychostimulant medication was actually indicated. Now, lacking this evaluation, many pediatricians are prescribing such medications because mothers or teachers have spoken the term *hyperactive*.

This same problem exists with the detection and treatment of childhood depression. How is a pediatrician to know the true mental status of a child without a legitimate evaluation? As a result, childhood depression is seldom suspected; if it is, an antidepressant is prescribed without proper indications or follow-up. In the past several years, we have lost almost everything many dedicated people have brought to the mental-health profession in this country. Thanks to managed care, there is essentially no mental-health system left, especially for children.

The failure of managed care has also affected what should be a very important day in the life of a child—the first day of first grade. If a child has psychological or potential academic problems that are not corrected or compensated for before the first grade, that child will have difficulties for years to come. Before the decline of mental-health care, we earnestly recommended that every child have a complete psychological and academic exam prior to entering first grade. This way we were able to identify almost any potential problem that child might have and either correct it or make sure that it would be handled appropriately. When such problems go undetected, they will most assuredly end in tragic results for the child and the parents.

While I strongly recommend a complete evaluation for every child, I know the difficulties so many parents will encounter. Because most insurance companies will not pay for this, and because competent child psychiatrists and child psychologists are consequently having a hard time providing for their own families, the art of psychological/academic evaluations for children is fast disappearing. The best I can suggest is to try to find one of these rapidly disappearing evaluators who will give your child such an evaluation, even if you have to pay for it yourself. The most important advantage of this is that you will be able to plan for your child's educational future, and if any tendencies toward problems are found, you will know what they are and be able to take care of them.

A FINAL WORD

The topics in this chapter can be troubling. You certainly don't need to develop excessive anxiety while worrying about whether your child will do so. Remember that as a parent, there is a limitless amount of positive power available to you. You have the opportunity to provide love and tender care every single day. If you keep that emotional tank full and give special attention to training your child in anger management, your chances of avoiding some of these challenges are tremendously higher.

Even so, we all are imperfect creatures. You and I have experienced many bumps in the road on our paths toward mature adulthood. Your child will have the same mixture of steps and stumbles. Take the child's hand, help him or her understand how deep and permanent your love is, and walk together down that path, with confidence that God is going to give you the guidance and wisdom you need at every bend in the road.

I've counseled many families and many children over the years, and I know that no matter how worrisome the problems may be as they arise, no question is without an answer. There is always some wise and loving step you can take. You'll be up to the task. You want to be a terrific parent, or you wouldn't be reading a book about the subject. I hope you never encounter depression or intensified anxiety in your children, but if so, we are fortunate to live in an age of effective treatments and to live in the light of knowing that God uses even the toughest experiences to help us grow and flourish.

9 THE KEY TO MOTIVATION

MOTIVATION IS A CURIOUS THING. Everyone knows what it is—we can describe it simply as the "want to" that is required to accomplish something. The greatest accomplishments of your life have come when you were highly motivated. And every morning when you struggle to face another day at the office or cleaning the house, you understand that the problem is lack of motivation.

But few people understand how it works; it is an elusive and complex topic. There is an old story about a man who moved to a quiet neighborhood to enjoy his retirement. For several weeks, his afternoons were calm and delightful. Then three bored teenagers began hanging out a few doors down, kicking garbage cans just for the enjoyment of making noise.

The man gave it a little thought. Then he went to talk to the kids. He shook their hands and said, "I see you're doing what I used to enjoy when I was your age—kicking garbage cans! I still love to hear it, so I hope you won't stop. I'll tell you what I'll do: I'll pay each of you a dollar a week just to come kick these cans for a few minutes every day."

The teenagers were overjoyed. A dollar a week just to kick some grubby old garbage cans! They received their dollar for two weeks, then the man appeared again. "Boys, I just want to tell you you're doing a great job," he said. "But I'm on a fixed income, and my bills are increasing. I'm going to have to cut your pay to fifty cents per week."

The boys were a little disappointed, but they kept on kicking. The following week the man reported another pay cut. He hoped his young friends could continue their great work for a quarter per week. The three teenagers looked at one another and said, "No way! We're not kicking any more cans for a lousy quarter!"

From that day on, the man enjoyed the resumption of peace and quiet in the neighborhood. It would seem he knew at least one secret of motivating young people. How can you motivate your own children?

MOTIVATION: THE BASICS

One sixth-grade boy reads a book every two or three days. He enjoys his reading, but he admits he would never get through so many volumes if his school didn't have an accelerated reader program. This system awards points for every book read. The child takes a brief test to prove he read the book, and he competes against other readers for small prizes. It's a good example of motivating a youngster toward a good and healthy habit. We would hope that sooner or later he'll read not for a superficial reward but because he enjoys reading and feels that his life is enriched by the experience.

Yet another boy in his class may not be motivated by the same program. It may take some other approach entirely to get him to read, to study, or to work harder on getting along with fellow students. We see children who are highly motivated toward various established goals; we see others who can never seem to stay on task and finish an assignment. Most boys and girls fall somewhere in the middle. Motivation levels in children are related to both natural aptitudes and personal attitudes. Other factors are health, energy, training, and even chemical or biological differences in the minds of children.

Perhaps even more important, we want to think about not only *whether* children are motivated but *how.* It's possible to see a child motivated for all the wrong reasons, and the end results can be very negative. Our first insight about motivation is that there are both conscious and unconscious factors. In an earlier chapter, we compared a human being to a city with visible landmarks (buildings, people, activity) as well as "invisible" networks (pipes, wires, cables, even politics) that really influence the life and health of the city. People, too, are more than they seem on the outside; there are many subtle, hidden factors that influence decisions. When we see a child—or anyone, for that matter—act in ways that seem irrational, it's a good bet that unconscious elements inspire the behavior. There might be anger, guilt, or some remnant of a past emotion or powerful influence.

Most of us assume that our decisions are the result of calm, rational thought processes that weigh the positives and negatives before selecting the right choice. Life would be extremely more pleasant for all of us if that were true! Far more often than we know, however, less rational factors guide our decisions. The motivations can be complex; they can be the result of some long-forgotten incident or impulse.

Some subconscious motivations have genetic origins: shyness or playfulness, for example. But I believe that for most of us, the majority come from experiences early in life. Perhaps an adult has a deep fear of insects because of some childhood experience, for example. During the first few years of life, events and experiences are affecting us far more profoundly. This is the time when we are learning the vast bulk of the important knowledge of life. We have seen that some thought processes will become powerful while others will be abandoned from disuse. It is during this very period that parents have the most influence over their children. Therefore, the conclusion is clear: Parents can largely manage the unconscious factors that will powerfully guide a child's decisions and perceptions throughout life. The love you offer and the love you withhold on any given day are emotional investments in your child that will reap positive or negative dividends for many decades. That is, good and loving parenting creates positive subconscious motivations in children from the very beginning. We have a once-in-their-lifetime opportunity in those early years.

And as we will see, we discover two keys to their motivation.

Wanting and Feeling

My wife is the most positively motivated person I've ever known. She always seems to be well focused on the important things in life, and she stays busy getting them done. But the key is that she enjoys herself every step of the way. Whether it's chairing a committee at church, working around the home, or volunteering on some service project, she is a happy whirlwind of activity. Naturally, churches, schools, and other organizations recognize these qualities right away and do all they can to keep her busy. She never waits until the last minute to get her work done; she never does anything out of pressure or guilt. And of course, whatever she does, she does well, because she's pleased to be doing it.

I wish I could make the same observations about myself! I tend to procrastinate over projects, worrying about the details and whether or not I'll do a good job. Then I derive less enjoyment from my work, because I feel stressed by the deadlines and the pressure. Obviously, Pat is a much better model of the motivated life. And why? I think there are two keys to the presence of positive motivation. First, there is desire—the "want to." Then there is something subtler: feelings. Think of the times you've been highly motivated. Perhaps it was to date or marry a certain individual. Perhaps it was to get that dream job or dream house. You can probably feel the high emotions that were connected to what you desired.

Positively motivating our children, therefore, is all about their wanting the right things for the right reasons. Do you want your child to feel motivated to eat vegetables through fear of illness or through a pleasant desire to be healthy and strong? Do you want your child to have good homework habits to avoid punishment or for the pleasure of an all-As report card? Motivations are all about motives—what we want, fueled by what we feel.

What happens when people do the right things for the wrong reasons? We can look around us today and see a world filled with people acting from negative motivations. People struggle to meet obligations of all kinds, from work assignments to family tasks, because they learned as children to be motivated by pressure, rewards, threats, punishment, or guilt. We recognize the "What's in it for me?" attitude in those not motivated by right but by reward. How often do we see anyone act sacrificially simply because it's right and it brings them joy, rather than from some negative motive?

The few positively motivated among us—people like my wife, Pat, and my grown children—seem to have something rare and wonderful at the core of their souls. This attribute is *optimism*. The pessimists surround us, of course, so that when we come across a true optimist we are almost startled. These are people who always see the possibility of a positive solution, and that certainty draws them forward with energy and resolve. Can you imagine a better description for the kind of person you want your child to grow into?

The optimist fails but instinctively believes the challenge can still be met; there's an external solution waiting to be found. The pessimist, on the other hand, tends to see the failure inside herself: "This went wrong because there's something wrong with me."

And how do we become one or the other? Some of it is a matter of temperament and could be genetic. But much of it is learned through experience, particularly in the early years. The child who succeeds in the early challenges will have greater confidence in those that follow for the rest of his life. He will bounce back from failure with a can-do attitude and a resiliency that will keep feeding its own positive energy.

What we want, then, is to help our children believe in themselves and their abilities early on, to feel secure and loved so that they can move forward at the right times, and to learn to act from personal confidence and the joy of prevailing. This is the power of positively motivated children.

Leading the Way

Laying the groundwork for positive motivation begins with your own example. Learning comes most often from modeling, and the first and most significant models are our own parents. How did your own mother and father attack problems? What basic goals motivated them? You can bet that the answers soaked into you, too.

Many of us subconsciously understand our own motivations and feel they're the right ones, so we pass them on. But that's an important issue. Are you teaching your children the best and most positive motivations or simply the ones that have driven you? Ed was raised by a stern and demanding father who demanded good schoolwork and excellent behavior. The alternatives were thoroughly unpleasant, so Ed got the best grades and behaved well at home. Today he finds himself telling his own son, "My father would never have accepted a grade like this one! . . . If you had ever acted up like that in his home, you'd have been out by the woodshed before you could blink!"

Even if he doesn't take his own children outside for corporal punishment, it's clear he is thinking about and drawing from his own raising. But is he using the most positive motivation or passing on the fears and threats he came by honestly?

You'll want to lead and train your children with a relaxed, loving, positive, dedicated example that communicates, "Life works best when I'm responsible and dedicated to the right things." If they see procrastination, they're likely to take on that trait. If they see guilt-based performance, they'll pick it up, too. But if you begin with love, keeping their emotional tanks filled, they'll identify with you and want to be as much like you as possible.

At one time I worked with the Operation Head Start program, showing teachers this love principle. They would bring me an example of a three-year-old child suffering from fear and anxiety. I knew the basis of the problem: emotional deprivation. I made my point by asking the teachers to first teach the child something by sitting across from them at the table. Then I told them to try teaching them something else—while holding the child and making occasional eye contact. The child learned far more rapidly when held. Why? Needs come first. As long as your child—or any child—has a love deficit, they cannot move forward and meet the challenges at the proper junctures. We saw the principle clearly played out in our brief time with Head Start children; how much more powerful is this concept in the days, months, and years you spend with your child?

Subconscious Anger

As a reverse example, I think of the awful trend of school violence and shootings we have seen since the late nineties. I was shocked by the media discussions as to why these tragedies occurred. Every reason from television to guns to music to video games was explored. No one brought up the real issue: negative subconscious motivation. Why else would children act so irrationally, walking into schools with loaded rifles? There was profound anger in these kids, yet it was hidden so well that teachers and parents had totally missed it; the kids themselves probably weren't aware of it. When we can't train our children in anger management, this kind of thing is inevitable. Kids feel unloved, they enter their natural adolescent period of passive aggression, and they act out their anger irrationally and primitively.

But the media "talking heads" never brought up anger management in my hearing. What they did discuss was their puzzlement over the supposedly "good homes" many of these children came from. What they meant was that affluent, middle-class, even churchgoing families were producing schoolroom violence. Subconscious motivations, of course, fail to distinguish any meaningful differences between affluent and impoverished homes, even between religious and nonreligious households.

This is why we've seen so many Christian parents suddenly wondering "where they went wrong" as parents. Many of them, without realizing it, have used behavior modification–based training. They have used stern discipline and perhaps corporal punishment, because over the last couple of decades these supposedly "traditional" approaches to training have been in vogue. But behavior-mod parenting is reactive rather than proactive. Overly strict parents suddenly find themselves with adolescent children filled with passive-aggressive anger. The kids are striking out at parents, authority, church, and every value they perceive they were expected to adopt. Yet Mom and Dad did it by the book—Christian books. What happened?

What happened was that harsh, power-based parenting created a resentment that had to go underground. It became stealth anger, simmering to a boil all the while Mom and Dad thought things were going well. The anger *had* to be hidden because of fear of reprisal. But the inevitable time would come when the anger would be acted out dramatically.

The Key to Motivation

BEHAVIOR AND POSITIVE MOTIVATION

How, then, can we guide and train our children without creating anger and resentment? Let's review our earlier material on the five ways to control a child's behavior. You'll recall that two of them are positive, two are negative, and one is neutral. In the light of our subject of motivation, they bear revisiting:

Requests (Positive)

When we ask our children to take an action, we're sending several useful messages. We're saying, "I respect your feelings." We're saying, "I respect your opinions about this matter." Children can see that they are being approached as mature individuals, and they are more likely to respond positively. But the most important message we are sending is, "I expect you to take responsibility for your own behavior." That in itself is a way of moving your child one step closer to emotional and psychological maturity.

Commands (Negative)

Commands are necessary at times even if negative. Children won't always respond to a polite request. We have to keep in mind that the message of a command is, "Your feelings and your opinions are not important here." And in contrast to the request, we are saying, "I don't expect you to take responsibility for your own behavior. I simply expect you to do what I tell you to do." While we all command our children at times—ideally in a gentle but firm manner—we want to remember that a steady diet of command-based parenting creates resentment. It reinforces again and again a feeling of powerlessness in the child, a feeling of having feelings and opinions that are ignored. And again, the child will not learn to take responsibility for himself, only to do what is absolutely demanded.

Gentle Physical Manipulation (Positive)

In this approach we take the child in a nonthreatening way and move him toward the goal we desire. There are times when we need to be more demonstrative than simply using speech. We take a young child's hand and walk him to the bedroom at his bedtime. Or in the case of an older child, say, a teenager in emotional turmoil in the midst of some dispute, we gently put an arm around his shoulder and say, "Come on, let's take a walk." Then we go to another room or perhaps outdoors and say, "Let's just sit here awhile." The approach is more active and less resistible than a verbal request, but it still sends the same positive messages, offering respect and allowing the child to take personal responsibility.

Punishment (Negative)

One great problem about punishment is that it's always difficult to find the right level. What punishment is suitable? What is too much? Too little? If we are too lenient, the child doesn't learn the truth about the consequences of his actions. If we are too strict, the child becomes angry and resentful. Punishment is sometimes necessary, of course, but as the most negative control method, it must be attended to with care.

Behavior Modification (Neutral)

At special times we may use positive or negative reinforcement (reward or penalty) to motivate our children. There might be some truly special goal, for example, that is worthy of special motivation. "If you make all As on your report card, I'll take you for an all-day trip to the amusement park." We would do this as a supplement to the normal positive encouragement to be a good student. Or in a more negative situation, it might be appropriate in the case of a son with a bad habit to establish a jar where he must donate a quarter every time he belches in front of the family. But what happens when reward and punishment dominate all parental training? We find ourselves with grown children who are very angry and who will take no action without the promise of a reward.

NEGATIVE MOTIVATION

Motivation uses energy. In the case of negative subconscious motivation, guilt, fear, and pressure will absorb a great deal of a child's energy. But as we give our children what they need emotionally, then motivate them positively, we energize them. We empower them to be successful and fruitful in life.

Sadly, many parents fail to motivate their children in the right way. They pass on some of the mistakes by which they were raised, or they take some other well-meaning but misguided approach. Let's examine four of the most common negative motivations.

Passive Aggression

We have already examined "stealth anger" in detail. I believe it to be one of the most destructive forces in our world. It can certainly ruin the life of your child as well as the lives of friends and family in his immediate circle. This is an unrecognized force that finally breaks loose, causing the child to act irrationally through behavior in a way that hurts the angry one most of all. Make anger management a priority in your parenting.

Insecurity

What we're mainly referring to here is the constant need to prove or justify one's worth. What happens if a child comes to believe that she is loved on the basis of her actions? That she must perform to be considered an acceptable human being? There are many people out there today who live with this terrible, constant burden of proof. And what I find most tragic of all is that it all tends to originate in a household where Mom and Dad did indeed love their child unconditionally—they simply never figured out that they needed to make that crystal clear, or they never figured out *how.* Just remember that your child can never be too loved or too accepted. Fill that emotional tank so your child will be free to perform for personal joy and contentment, rather than for a desperate and unending pursuit of worthiness.

Guilt

Let's focus for a minute on your quiet, well-behaved child—the shy one who never gave you a minute's trouble. This is your home's top candidate for the burden of guilt. He has a deep need to please you, and without realizing it, you will pick up on that fact and use it to your advantage. This child lives to please authority figures and has a deep fear of falling short in that goal. No matter how worthy it may seem, guilt is another wrong motivation. Think about what happens when your child falls under the spell of the wrong authority figure. Stronger-minded, controlling figures will exploit your child's innocent desire to please. His need is to become self-sufficient, to work for the rewarding inner goals that give us contentment rather than someone else's goals. He is good at caring and compassion; help him know that he need not be perfect to be loved.

Pressure

How many of us have said, "I do my best work under pressure"? Perhaps this is because our parents used high pressure to get results from us. We pressure our children through disapproval, through anger, or through the threat of punishment. The anxiety and fear, of course, drive children toward the desired results—but they are very destructive motivations. As we've seen in our previous chapter on anxiety and depression, the results can be devastating. Your child may be more productive with pressure today, but in the long run he will actually be less productive. He may finally find himself paralyzed, incapable of performing. Children have enough anxiety today. We need not add to that.

LEARNING TO LEARN

There are several basic truths we need to keep in mind as we guide our children through the earliest learning experiences and on to the challenges of school.

First, we need to know that during childhood, children are motivated to learn the basics of life. They are hungry for learning during these early years. Simply watch a child at play, and you'll see that every moment involves some kind of experimentation, some attempt to learn something new. Children respond to every stimulus with wide eyes and open ears, ready to take in information. We need to realize that children come with the motivation built in. All we need to do is engage it effectively and positively.

Second, we need to realize that a child will move forward at his level at the proper time *if* his emotional needs are met—that is, if he is secure and loved. Some parents are in a hurry to teach their children to read or to learn numbers. They become so caught up in teaching, they forget that even more than the parent's information, the child wants the assurance of the parent's love—particularly if some difficult new task is being presented. Your child is thinking, What if I can't do this? Is it still okay? Will Mommy or Daddy withhold their love? Take care of that need early and often, and your child will respond effectively to your teaching.

Third, our greatest goal in teaching our children is that of moving them from our control to self-control. The greatest lesson of all is personal responsibility. Keep in mind that *two people cannot take responsibility for the same thing at the same time.* Parents—mothers in particular—tend to become anxious about their children getting homework done, for example. They will hover over their child, check every paper, and make sure every book and pencil is properly placed in the child's backpack.

Schoolwork and Readiness

Keep in mind the wonderful principle that is always on your side: Younger children want to learn. The motivation comes preinstalled in each child. From the first few months, your child will be learning something new almost momentarily, hungrily absorbing new sensations and new data from her eyes, ears, taste, touch, and smell. There is a right kind of learning for each new stage, and you need only be certain your child is ready to learn at the right time. You can do that by filling emotional needs, for a child who needs love will never be ready to learn. And just as there are levels of cognitive (mental) readiness, there are levels of emotional maturity that need to keep pace. It's more than taking in new information, you see; your child needs to be at the right level for controlling anxiety, withstanding stress, and maintaining personal equilibrium in her small, ever-changing world. Fill her emotional tank so it will be ready to fill her hungry mind.

Then, of course, comes the issue of schoolwork. Sometime during the grade-school years, homework becomes a classic challenge for many parents. *How can I be sure my child gets his homework done?* By this time in our lives, we as adults have come to understand the critical nature of taking care of daily responsibilities. We have assignments at the office, cooking and cleaning at home, and church and neighborhood responsibilities that are pressing all the time. We've hopefully reached an adult level of maturity concerning our responsibilities. But our children haven't reached that level; they haven't learned that lesson. And many of them tend to procrastinate, to forget to write down what the homework assignment is, or to simply lose focus when they arrive home—children are tired from the day just as we are.

There is one central truth to remember at all times:

> Two persons cannot take responsibility for the same task at the same time.

Yes, I know it's hard to stand by as your child fails to dot every *i* and cross every *t* as you would do. But you can't afford to intervene and take on the responsibility of your child's homework, because you'll be robbing your child of a critical lesson that must be personally, individually learned. Remember, he is moving from your control to self-control. Reclaiming your control at the first moment of uncertainty retards that progression; it keeps your child childish when it comes to the lesson of personal responsibility. You need to hover and keep watch a little less each day, allowing your child to take a little more responsibility—stand or stumble.

And if you want your child to be healthily and positively motivated, remember this:

> When your child takes the initiative in his assignments, he is taking responsibility; when he takes responsibility, he is motivated.

There comes a time for nearly every child when homework completion becomes an issue—particularly during what we call the normal passive-aggressive period of early adolescence. Even then, you need to remember that homework is not only your child's responsibility but your child's own lesson in maturity. So what can you do? You can mention that you'll be happy to help with the homework, as long as that doesn't mean taking the pencil and paper and doing the work yourself. If your child is struggling with a mathematics concept, for example, you can help find where in the textbook that skill is explained and encourage your child to study that segment again. Don't fall into the trap of having to sit by every day while your child does his work. He will quickly learn to manipulate you into thinking he cannot work, or cannot concentrate, unless you're nearby.

What if, in reading this page, you discover that you already need to pull back from your involvement in your child's homework preparation? Be prepared for the thing you dread: a drop in grades that will hopefully be temporary. This is how your child will learn what responsibility means; sometimes the hard way is the only way we learn the important lessons. Learning to be self-sufficient is a lesson that must be learned by your child, and must be learned well. Don't short-circuit the process simply to curb your own anxiety.

SPECIAL INTERESTS

There remains one final issue in our discussion of motivation. It's a wonderful day when you begin to identify special talents and interests in your child. There will be a number of these, because children are eager and interested on every front. There will be new passions and hobbies that fall by the wayside, but there will also be special loves and abilities that take root and abide throughout life. You want to encourage your child to pursue those interests in the right direction, particularly in a context where there is so much competition (much of it empty) for your child's attention: television, computer games, and so forth.

As we've seen, the minds of children are laying circuitry that will last. They're "hard-wiring" some patterns and rejecting others. How tragic for afternoon television, for example, to be part of that permanently established mental framework. That's why you want to encourage your child to develop her skills in music, art, athletics, or special fields of interest.

It's not easy to choose the best activities. On the one hand, perhaps you wish your parents had encouraged you to stick with piano lessons or Scouting. On the other hand, you understand that forcing a child's participation can create anger and rebellion. Therefore, motivation is the key. You want your child to want the right things.

We'll stay with piano for our example. Whet your child's appetite in creative ways. Play piano music for her and point out some of the wonderful styles—jazz, classical, rock, and so on. If you know a little piano yourself, you can put your child's fingers on the keys and show her how to make a chord and how different chords change the melody and the feeling. At church or school, take your child up to the piano when a good musician is playing it. Encourage the child to ask questions.

At some point, your child (if she truly has some natural gifts in that area) will want to talk about piano lessons. As you discuss this, act as if you're doing her a big favor with the lessons—the idea is that this is something for her and a special treat, not something you're lobbying for. At all times, remember that when it becomes "your thing" instead of "her thing," the magic will be gone. You might be tempted to reward loyalty to piano lessons, for example, but the problem is that you're replacing, as the goal, a reward rather than the joy of the pursuit itself. She needs to be motivated by her own attraction to the pleasure of learning piano. When the motivation or the responsibility of the lessons swings over to you, piano lessons will come to resemble a chore in her eyes.

The initiative, then, comes from your child—and when you give praise to her efforts, that praise is truly meaningful instead of one more part of your lobbying process. The child must "own" the pursuit of the piano, or of whatever special interest she is pursuing.

That's the best way to help your child pursue the special

interests that add color and individuality to life and personhood. Look for the areas that naturally attract your child, let
her have the opportunities to explore that attraction and
develop her skills, and let her lead the way with initiative that
fuels desire and motivation.

SUMMING IT UP

Motivation is such an important concept for your child and
your parenting. It takes special care, special wisdom, and just
the right touch of loving guidance to keep your child motivated in all the right ways toward all the right goals. Be certain
that you yourself are constantly motivated. A wonderful model
is found in Paul's words in Philippians 3:12–14:

> Not that I have already obtained all this, or have already been
> made perfect, but I press on to take hold of that for which
> Christ Jesus took hold of me. Brothers, I do not consider
> myself yet to have taken hold of it. But one thing I do:
> Forgetting what is behind and straining toward what is
> ahead, I press on toward the goal to win the prize for which
> God has called me heavenward in Christ Jesus.

Imagine sitting in Roman captivity as the apostle was, with
every impulse pushing you to see the world and spread the
gospel. He had so much to do and so little opportunity.
Shouldn't that have choked his desire and extinguished the
flame of his motivation? Not in Paul's case. As we see in these
verses, he was absolutely confident that God was doing something uniquely within and through his life. Imprisonment
guaranteed that he would have to write letters to the churches

he loved, and God then used those letters to instruct Christians through the centuries.

Paul didn't bemoan his fate or worry about what had gone wrong. He forgot what was behind, strained for what was ahead, and pushed to take hold of the goal for which God had taken hold of him. That attitude has everything to do with good parenting. Just as Paul's heavenly Father nurtured within him the desire and the feelings to accomplish all the right goals in life—to become everything he was designed by God to become—your heavenly Father motivates you to train your children lovingly, graciously, and positively. Life may be difficult, but it is also filled with beauty, pleasure, and the sheer joy of serving God and others. As your children see these attributes in you—as they see that unquenchable thirst for the best in life—they will follow your lead with all their hearts. As you are motivated to "win the prize," so will they be.

For Paul, the wellspring of motivation, of happiness, of continuing wisdom and accomplishment was simply *love*—love for God and love for others. Let that same love rule your household, and you will raise wonderful, motivated children who will make the world a better place for their presence and the parenting you and your Lord have provided.

10 Q AND A WITH DR. C.

As you complete this book, there may still be one question on your lips: "But what about . . ."

As I've counseled so many families over the years, I've naturally discovered a number of constants, a number of universals, a number of recurring themes. As a matter of fact, you should be comforted to know that whatever specific challenge may stand before you now, it is something many other parents are facing.

We close this volume with a collection of questions that parents have frequently brought to me:

Q: *I'm interested in this area of physical touch. You say that an important way to fill my child's emotional tank is by showing love. But I have a teenage son who seems uncomfortable when I try to touch him. How do I lovingly touch a child who recoils from touch?*

ROSS: You'll need to be very discerning and sensitive, but don't give up on your efforts to touch your child. Let me offer you a few suggestions:

- Be casual. Casually tap his leg or shoulder while you're laughing at the television. Be nonchalant about it; in general, you'll be more successful when you're not making a big deal out of touching.

- Touch your son when he is upset and needs comfort; barriers will be down then, too.

- Touch when you have something important to say. When his friend has called on the phone and you've answered, smile and tap him on the shoulder as you hand him the receiver, rather than yelling down the hall.

- Gentle pats on the back and simple high-fives might work for your son.

- A simple touch when passing in the hall, or when your son is distracted by something else, will go over without protest. Even when he doesn't know he's been touched, the physical contact registers with his body and communicates the same positives.

- Just keep in mind that even when our children superficially resist, they want and need the love that physical touch communicates—and it will soothe and encourage more than they expect it will. Teenagers are in the process of trying to work out what they do and don't want, but let's be certain we give them the basics of love that they always need. Adolescents naturally withdraw a bit, but don't let that be the occasion for withdrawing the vehicles of our nurture.

Q & A With Dr. C

Q: *I agree that we want to avoid the punishment trap, but your suggestion is to sit down and discuss what is appropriate with other parents or close friends. What about letting my child participate in the discussion?*

ROSS: It's a question of readiness in terms of emotional maturity. A younger child lacks the maturity to be objective in making decisions about her punishment. Involving her then would be a mistake. But a more mature child understands the rationale behind punishment. She also understands the nuances of the "punishment fitting the crime." Let such a child gradually take part in the discussion and the decision making—understanding, of course, that the parents must always retain the final authority.

As we've seen, the journey is one from parental control to self-control. During the teenage years, you should gradually shift from your control to your trust. To the extent that a teenager demonstrates trustworthiness, you award him with appropriate liberties. For example, if he has gotten in some trouble outside the home, you'll be far less lenient about letting him stay out late. But if he has been a well-behaved and responsible child, you will let him participate in deciding how late he may stay out on a weekend. It's a judgment call all the way, and you have to be wise and thoughtful in making for a smooth transition from your control to the child's trustworthy self-control.

My book *How to Really Love Your Teenager* carries a more in-depth discussion of this issue.

Q: *I'd like to hear a little more about the punishment trap. Why do so many children fall into it?*

ROSS: For one thing, authoritative, reactive parenting has been the trend over the last generation—particularly with the evangelical crowd. Recently I've observed that there is a relationship between works-oriented faith and the desire to use behavior-mod, reward-and-punishment-based parenting. What I mean by that is, despite our Bible's teachings about God's wonderful grace, we in the church have a tendency to put everything right back in terms of works and *earning* our status of righteousness. We are "righteous" only because God declares us forgiven through Christ's sacrifice—but still, throughout the history of our faith, we have had a tendency to make faith a set of rules. Now if we (wrongfully) say, "God will love me *if. . .*," we will then tend to communicate to our children, "I will love you *if. . .*" If it's difficult to live out a New Testament, grace-based faith, it's just as difficult to live out a parenthood by grace. It's far easier (and more harmful) to institute an Old Testament, wrath-driven, punishment-based faith.

We've already discussed the fact that many people are misusing the Scriptures in their punishment-based parenting. They quote "Spare the rod and spoil the child" from Proverbs, but they forget that the rod was primarily an instrument of comfort and guidance, not chastisement.

I also think we have certain myths about the "good old days" when our grandparents walked the earth. We yearn for simple answers to today's complex problems, and we tend to misperceive that the "good old days" were simpler times. Yes, there were many wonderful aspects of that bygone culture. But if it did indeed produce superior children, the reason is not that children were taken out to the woodshed more often but that children were more affectionately loved and their emotional needs were better met.

Q: *I find it difficult as a parent not to simply lean on my power and authority by saying things like, "Because I said so!" How can I respond in a basic humility without losing my authority?*

ROSS: That's a great question. We need to remember that meekness is not weakness but the process of using power and authority maturely. It is not the same as being permissive, and it does not amount to giving up your authority.

Think of the example of Jesus, who was meek and humble yet powerful and authoritative. His actions were always rooted in love and service. In the wilderness, his three temptations all involved misusing his power. But he never gave in to the kind of traps that tempt us.

Meekness is feeling angry at our children yet not raising our voices or venting our emotions—a common misuse of power, because we are modeling to our children an action we forbid in them. When your child sees you exercising self-control, your humility and proper use of power will be admired. Meekness is also about the general respect with which you approach your children. When you have time for them, when you talk with them and joke with them, and when you serve as friend as well as parent—on those occasions your children will perceive you as humble and approachable, and your authority will be strengthened rather than forfeited.

Q: *There is so much conflicting advice for me as a parent. How do I know I'm on the right track? How can I know I'm doing a good job while there's time to make corrections?*

ROSS: First of all, the fact that you're reading this book (and that you've gotten this far) says a lot about your desire to be a great parent. Any parent who truly loves his or her children enough to want to be a great parent can do so.

I would recommend periodically asking yourself three questions:

1. What are my motives as a parent? Are they to instill maturity, wisdom, and responsibility?
2. What are my priorities as a person? Are there pursuits in my life that come before my home, my spouse, and my children?
3. What is the atmosphere in my home? Is it primarily positive and loving, or is it negative and conflict-driven?

When things aren't going well, you'll know it by a negative atmosphere and a feeling that you and your child are at cross-purposes. If that's the case in your home now, you'll want to make some changes. Read through this book (a second time, if necessary) and ask yourself which chapters pegged the main issues in your home. Are there anger problems? Motivational issues?

Whatever the case may be, it's always helpful to get back to the basics: providing unconditional love and acceptance. If you can say with certainty that such a loving atmosphere is established in your home, the solutions to your problems are within reach.

Q: *The issue that stands out in our home is anger management. I would really like more guidance on that subject. Also, can you explain the Anger Ladder in more detail?*

ROSS: Many parents have your experience: the realization that anger is a tremendously critical issue. There is no way to cover all the angles of this subject in the short chapter we've provided, but I've written a full book on the subject: *How to Really Love Your Angry Child*. I would highly recommend that you get a copy and study it closely if anger is an unresolved issue in your home. Nothing has greater power to derail the life of your child, and hurt many other people besides, than poorly managed anger.

The Anger Ladder is simply a visual illustration that shows our desired progress from the worst and most harmful responses to those that represent maturity and wisdom in managing anger. No one ever becomes perfect in this pursuit, and we all have room for improvement. But the top of the ladder shows the goal to keep before you and your children: the ability to handle anger *verbally* and *pleasantly*. You won't reach the finish line all at once; most of us find we can handle anger verbally long before that hardest part, handling it pleasantly. But when you reach that goal, you will have transformed anger (in your life or the life of your child) from a ticking time bomb to a positive factor that is actually useful and enriching. For when we deal with tense issues verbally and pleasantly, we are likely to deal with those same issues effectively; and we're likely to deepen our relationship with that other person, rather than offending them through poorly handled anger.

Q: *Ross, I was very interested in what you said about your house becoming a favorite hangout for your children's friends. That's a very appealing goal for us. How can we make our home a comfortable place for teens and their friends? What activities do you recommend, other than television and video games, that would make our kids' friends want to spend time with us?*

ROSS: This was something my wife, Pat, and I thought about early on, as our kids approached adolescence. We designed our house to provide a space for our children, and we furnished it with games like Ping-Pong and pool.

I also took the time and energy to get to know our children's friends and their parents. It helped us to know all that we could about these kids, their problems, their interests, and what kind of homes they lived in. In the case of the church youth group, we found that goal quite simple; for other kids, it took a bit more work. Parents' meetings for sports, as well as school functions, helped us. The important thing was making a priority of getting to know our children's friends and being available for them to know us.

When the teenage years arrived, we made it very clear to our kids that they should feel free to have their friends in our home whenever possible. One way to show we meant this was to provide food—that's not a bad way to make your house attractive to teenagers, by the way. When there were school, team, or church events, kids knew our home was a great "stopover" afterward.

Finally, when our kids' friends were in our home, we didn't disappear. We tried to spend time with each individual, talking, asking questions, and building relationships. At times we were able to provide a listening ear and a little extra comfort and love to kids who often needed it and may have had problems communicating with their own parents. We have found that as the years have gone by, many of these relationships have endured.

Q: *You said that a child won't be motivated to learn if his emotional needs are unfilled. Are love and learning really that tightly connected? What about a gifted child with a high IQ and healthy curiosity?*

ROSS: Remember that we are *whole* people. All that is

inside us is integrated, so that body, soul, mind, and spirit each have their effect on the others. An IQ is not a fixed item. It, too, flourishes or suffers based on the variable of emotional needs. An unloved child will experience a falling IQ and an increasing ambivalence toward loving.

Curiosity is no different. Well-loved, well-balanced children are curious, energetic, and eager. Children with unmet emotional needs become inner-directed and less curious. They lack the emotional energy that fuels curiosity. Emotional health, in summary, is just as important as innate IQ when it comes to the ability to learn.

Q: *What are some positive ways to use the media?*

ROSS: First of all, know the treasures from the trash. It has been observed that there is actually more quality children's programming than at any time in the past—it's just that there's also much more harmful content. Any television, DVD player, or VCR can be a help to the parent if the right content is screened. The key is to record what is good and make it available during your child's viewing time. As your children grow older and more sophisticated (as well as more curious about what their school friends are watching), look for older shows such as *The Andy Griffith Show;* many of these types of shows are positive and show good value systems. Also help your children appreciate classic older movies—films by directors such as Frank Capra *(It's a Wonderful Life),* whose works are wholesome but still very entertaining.

Fredrica, a second-grade teacher from Pensacola, Florida, told us about a special child who treated both adults and other children with wonderful courtesy. Fredrica told her one day, "You have marvelous manners. You must come from a home where good manners are taught." The little girl explained that, actually, she got her manners from black-and-white movies! She went on to explain that she liked the way people treated one another in those old films.

We shouldn't be surprised, for study after study has shown that children imitate what they see on the screen. If they see Barney, they will imitate the purple dinosaur's behavior; if they watch superheroes, they will leap around and fight. Watch what your children watch, for what they see is what you'll get.

Q: *What about playing with children? Is that particularly important or helpful?*

ROSS: It has tremendous value. As a matter of fact, I feel a deep sense of loss over those old days of playing ball with my kids, going river rafting together, or simply playing indoor games on a rainy day. These are the times we are presenting the most powerful model for our children, for during these moments they enjoy us and identify with us the strongest. We create family memories that become powerful influences within the psyches of our children. Think of how much the Christmas traditions, the beach vacations, and the funny or unpredictable moments mean to you. These are shared memories that make a permanent bond and also tend to dissolve some of the anger or tensions that come naturally. In a way, the family that plays together stays together. Just this year I enjoyed a hiking trip through Scotland with nearly the whole clan, including grandchildren. I know that we can play together now because it's something we always did—and it's a natural expression of the love we have for one another.

11 PARTING WORDS

Sons are a heritage from the LORD,
  children a reward from him.
Like arrows in the hands of a warrior
  are sons born in one's youth.
Blessed is the man
  whose quiver is full of them. (Psalm 127:3–5)

W E CLOSE WITH THAT BEAUTIFUL IMAGE from the Psalms: the picture of the archer standing still, his eyes focused on the distant horizon, his bowstring fully extended and tense. The good archer can send his arrow far beyond the limits of his sight, and he can fire it with precision.

You are that archer, standing upright, eyes set on the future, sending your children on an arc toward the lofty goals you have for them. Doing the job right is not an easy or comfortable thing; it carries the tension of that bowstring, stretched to its very limit without snapping. If you've ever fired a bow, you know that it takes considerable strength and concentration. And you need good eyes as you fire that arrow into the distant forest.

But those children who fill your parental quiver are a "heritage from the LORD, . . . a reward from him." Without them, you would be like the archer without his arrows. How could you positively make an impact so far away?

Long after you are gone, your children will bear the powerful influence of all that you give them through your days of loving guidance. You will move on to an eternal reward, yet your children are one more way of living on in this world. It thrills us to realize that just as the arrow exceeds the archer, your children can go farther, accomplish greater things, and make a more lasting impact than you or your spouse has. Isn't that what each of us wants for our children? They are a heritage, and heritages can stretch for untold generations. What greater gift could God have placed in our hands? What is more worthy of the blood, the sweat, and the tears of our lives?

Strength, wisdom, impact, contentment—these are the things we want for our children. But what, in turn, do they want from *us*? A few years ago, George Barna conducted a poll to answer that very question.[1] Would you be surprised to hear that the very first item on the children's list was unconditional love? In their words, they wanted to be loved "no matter what." They wanted to feel "connected" to their parents. They wanted to be cherished for who they were.

Second, they wanted better communication—and specifically, deeper interaction on significant matters.

Third, they wanted more time and more focused attention.

Fourth, they wanted to be respected; they wanted to be afforded dignity.

Fifth, they wanted more purpose and meaning. They were highly interested in spiritually significant activities.

I think you may have noticed that the honest and candid responses of these children dovetail perfectly with the items we've discussed in this book. Our children want to be loved first and foremost. They don't want substitutes such as money or things. They don't want easy words. They want the real thing, and they want to feel as tightly connected with their parents as they were when they were babies.

They want their lives to have meaning and purpose. They want their families to have communication and interaction. They are pleading with us not to let them down—to be the loving parents who will make the difference in their lives.

On the other hand, what was their greatest fear? Divorce. Not only do they fear a physical separation of their parents, but they fear the emotional kind. Not only do they want to be cherished by Mom and Dad, but they want Mom and Dad to cherish each other. Perhaps the very thing that needs the most work in your parenting is the relationship between you and your spouse, for in the work of parenting, the archer never stands alone. It takes two to handle that bow.

So if you are a married parent, the two of you stand together, waiting for that right moment of release—the moment when your children are mature adults who will soar into the world on their appointed routes. But even if you are a single parent, know that your hands never grip that bow alone. There are greater hands than yours—the very hands that crafted you and your child. Raising a child without a parental partner is not the ideal. But your Lord will be by your side, giving you the wisdom and the strength that you need.

Whatever your situation, whatever your particular challenges, whatever problems have already beset your home, the future is always filled with hope. Our Lord wants us to succeed in our homes. He desperately wants our children to become a powerful and righteous generation. Toward that end, I know you will give all the love that you have to your child and become an encourager, strengthening your child every day as he or she moves toward the goal of being mature and filled with integrity.

Then, someday, you will stand at the throne of your Savior. Together you will look at the heritage that he gave you. Together you will see a bright path of good works in the world, a path of love and purpose. That will be the path of your children, the fruit of all your labor. And you'll see the smile on your Savior's face as he says, "Well done, my child. As I have loved you, so have you loved the children I gave you. Enter now into the rest and reward that await all those who have loved and served my children. And return now to the joy of the eternal home and the forever family."

FIVE WAYS TO GET THE MOST FROM THIS BOOK

1. Down the Block. Invite neighborhood parents for a weekly discussion over coffee, chapter by chapter. You'll enjoy building relationships on your street—and when the study is complete, your friends will find they've become a parental support group for advice and encouragement.

2. Over the Weekend. Have a "Moms' and Dads' Getaway" as a weekend retreat. Hit the book's key points for group sessions, small group interaction, and a closing time of prayer and commitment. A concentrated weekend focus on the material will give it extra impact, and you'll come home refreshed and rejuvenated, ready to apply your new understandings.

3. In the Classroom. Study a chapter per week with your adult Sunday school class. *How to Really Parent Your Child* can become a practical and rewarding class curriculum. Class members will enjoy comparing notes from their parenting experiences during the week—and reporting the week's progress in applying what they learn.

4. With Your Spouse. For a very personal one-on-one study experience, study each chapter with your spouse. Plan and protect an uninterrupted hour once or twice per week for reviewing the chapters and applying them to your household's special challenges. You'll grow together as a couple even as you grow into wiser parenthood.

5. Over the Internet. Start a "Real Parenting" bulletin board (such as a Google group or Yahoo group) and invite your friends to log on and share insights as they work through the book. Long after your study is finished, parents will want to continue sharing their experiences and assistance in your Web group.

STUDY GUIDE

Use this special chapter-by-chapter guide to enhance your growth as a parent. The questions are designed in such a way that you can use them in your personal study, in discussion with your spouse, or in a more formal group-learning experience.

Note the three kinds of questions provided:

1. Start. The first question for each chapter is a general (and gentle) way to begin thinking about the chapter's topic. It will help you or your group recall personal experiences that relate to what we'll be discussing. In a group session, this question is a good "icebreaker"—that is, it encourages participants to jump right into the discussion.

2. Study. These questions—five or more of them—move you through the main points of each chapter. Their goal is to help you not only clarify the key ideas but begin thinking about how they will help you as a parent.

3. Strengthen. Each chapter's final question will motivate you to consider how to put these truths to work during the next few days. These may be the most important questions of all, so if you study this book in a group setting, be certain you leave enough time to discuss the "strengthen" question.

INTRODUCTION:
LOST IN A STRANGE NEW WORLD

Start

1. What are some key ways that your children's daily world is different from the world of your own childhood?

Study

1. Edward Shorter offered three hallmarks of the "postmodern home." Which have you most observed? What are some of the root causes, in your opinion?

2. What is the wisest strategy for living in a "toxic" culture? What are some ways to do this?

3. What kind of transformation is called for in Romans 12:2? Explain what you think is involved in such a process.

4. What positive factors about this modern challenge should encourage us? What two factors does God always guarantee us?

5. What should be our most important goals for our children?

Strengthen

1. List or describe your current three greatest fears about

parenting. Based on the concepts mentioned in the introduction, how can you be more encouraged and effective as a parent this week?

CHAPTER ONE:
THE PARENTING CROSSROAD

Start

1. What has been the most surprising truth you have learned as a parent? If you could climb into a "time machine" and deliver one piece of advice to yourself at the point in time just before you became a parent, what would you say?

Study

1. In what ways does the task of parenting grow more complex, rather than simpler, as our children grow?
2. What is perspective, and how does it make a difference to us in considering the issues of parenting?
3. What are the long-term results of "reactive parenting"—that is, dealing with children based completely on their behavior at the moment?
4. What are the four essential need areas that all children share? Briefly explain each one.
5. Which of these four areas is most important? Which is most difficult?

Strengthen

1. Evaluate the four basic needs of children from the perspective of your own children. In which area do you need the most guidance? What can you do this week to improve in that area?

CHAPTER TWO:
BEGINNING WITH LOVE

Start

1. Is love "the greatest thing in the world," in your opinion? Why or why not? Why do you think it is so particularly critical in the home?

Study

1. Why is it that some children fail to comprehend that their parents love them?
2. What is the key difference in how parents and children communicate? What are some differences this distinction makes in our everyday lives?
3. What are three ways of using our behavior to express love? What is the importance of each?
4. What kind of atmosphere needs to be created in a home for good parenting to take place? Give examples of how this might be done.
5. What is the "emotional tank"? What are the basic ways of filling it?

Strengthen

1. Tomorrow, make it a point to use all three of the basic methods of filling your child's emotional tank. Take note of any difference in your child or the atmosphere of your household.

CHAPTER THREE:
BASIC TRAINING: THE DISCIPLINE PUZZLE

Start

1. What kind of discipline was used in your home when you were growing up? What were some of the positive and negative effects, in your opinion?

Study

1. How do reactive parents tend to approach the question of discipline? What are the results?
2. What difference does empathy make to a parent?
3. Discuss the importance of the control issue in a household. What are the two most common traps parents fall into?
4. What is the difference between discipline and punishment?
5. Discuss the five ways to control a child's behavior. How is each one positive, negative, or neutral?
6. According to Dr. Campbell, how can punishment remove guilt in an unhealthy way?

Strengthen

1. Reflect on how discipline is most often approached in your home. What improvements can you make next time?

CHAPTER FOUR:
THE POWER OF PROTECTION

Start

1. As a parent, what issues of protecting your child concern you the most? Why?

Study

1. For what reasons is it so important that we teach our children to think biblically and wisely?
2. What are the three basic ingredients of integrity? Which do you feel is most important? Why?
3. Why is it important to explain our thinking and reasoning to our children?
4. What are "I" messages? What makes this type of message effective?
5. Offer an example of a "teachable moment" from your experience. How can we watch for these moments?

Strengthen

1. How are you currently helping your child prepare for the challenges on his or her horizon? What can you do to help your child think clearly about what lies ahead?

CHAPTER FIVE:
DEFUSING THE ANGER EXPLOSION

Start

1. How was anger handled in your original home—through confrontation, avoidance, or discussion? Explain.

Study

1. Why is anger-management training "the most crucial and difficult task" for a parent?
2. What are the two vehicles for expressing anger? How does this relate to a child?
3. What are "unconscious" influences within us? Why might "stealth anger" be described as such?

4. Describe three factors that make stealth anger particularly troublesome.
5. What is the healthiest approach to handling angry emotions? What factors make this approach beneficial?
6. What is a "teachable moment"? Which of these suggestions do you find most helpful or important?
7. Why should we give so much attention to the concept of forgiveness in our homes?

Strengthen

1. Study the "Anger Ladder" diagram. Where would you most often place your own anger responses? Your spouse's? Your child's? What steps can you make to move to the next higher level?

CHAPTER SIX:
CONFRONTING THE MEDIA MONSTER

Start

1. Reflecting on your own growth years, what forms of popular culture played significant roles in your development? How so?

Study

1. What available evidence suggests that television molds behavior?
2. What influence has the growth of the Internet had on our culture? On your family?
3. For both television and computer activity, what is the most important restriction parents should make?
4. Why do remedies such as the V-chip and Internet filters often fail?

5. Since movie attendance takes place away from home, how can parents be aware of what their children are seeing?

Strengthen

1. Study the TV viewing guidelines near the conclusion of the chapter. Which ones can you put into practice today?

CHAPTER SEVEN:
NURTURING YOUNG SPIRITS

Start

1. Upon reflection, what are three goals you cherish in dreaming of your children's future as mature young adults?

Study

1. What is the single most important legacy we can pass on to our children? Why?

2. Why isn't verbal teaching enough when it comes to faith issues?

3. How does a child "fine-tune" the data he or she receives based on early experiences? What is the significance for our children's development?

4. What are some effective ways to create a spiritual atmosphere in the home?

5. Name some "tools for teaching" during the moments when our children look to us for faith. Which are most effective in your home?

Strengthen
1. Ask your children what they have learned about God in their home and how they have learned it. Spend some time sharing how faith has made a difference in your life.

CHAPTER EIGHT:
COPING WITH FEAR, ANXIETY, AND DEPRESSION
Start
1. What is your most prevalent fear related to your children? Why?

Study
1. What are the four basic fears parents face? Which do you think is most powerful?
2. What should parents remind themselves when they feel overcome with anxiety about parenting and their children?
3. How can anxiety be a useful thing? How can we balance the good forms with the bad?
4. What social factors have fueled tremendous increases in depression among young people?
5. What challenges are created by trends in managed care when it comes to treating anxiety disorders?
6. What indicators are most significant in helping us spot depression in our children?

Strengthen
1. Think carefully about the anxiety level in your home, remembering that this emotion is contagious. Who suffers the most anxiety? What kind of support needs

to be offered?

CHAPTER NINE:
THE KEY TO MOTIVATION

Start

1. What are the best motivational factors for you person-ally? What about your child?

Study

1. What is the most powerful—and least recognized—motivating force? Why are we so often unaware of it?
2. What roles do desire and emotions, respectively, play in motivation?
3. What is a crucial common denominator in those who seem to be positively motivated? What part does it play?
4. What is the danger of anger-driven motivation?
5. Review the five ways to control a child's behavior. Which are positive? Negative? Neutral? Which is (or are) preferable? Why?
6. Explain this concept: "Two people cannot take responsibility for the same thing at the same time."

Strengthen

1. Considering the points in this chapter, what do you feel is the best way to motivate your child? What steps can you take to do so?

Study Guide

FINAL EXAM

After reading this book, spend some time bringing all its key ideas together in your mind. Rereading the book is a great way to strengthen your comprehension and retention. You might also make a resolution to study the book every year or two and to discuss your progress with your spouse. For now, prayerfully and thoughtfully consider each of the questions below. Write out your answers and save them.

1. Turn to the contents page and review the chapter subjects. Which chapter had the greatest impact on you? Why?
2. Explain the most powerful conclusion you came to about your home and parenting from studying this book.
3. As you look at the key ideas, make a list of specific action steps for improving your effectiveness as a parent. Plan to begin carrying them out immediately.
4. Remember that parenting begins and ends with unconditional love and acceptance. Highlight this truth as your greatest goal, and look for ways to demonstrate this love every day.
5. A prayer to keep handy:

Lord, I often feel so humbled, so incomplete as I consider the responsibilities and demands of being a parent. What a power and a task to place in the small hands of a person like me! Yet I realize, too, that it is one more message that as I believe in you, you also believe in me—that even as you parent me in perfection, you trust me to parent in my own limited way, with your strong hand upon my shoulder.

I know the road will be tiring and filled with difficult turns. Yet you have promised your presence and your power, to supply every shred of wisdom and every needful resource. And so we will walk together through this valley; you as my Shepherd, this child as my sheep. Help me to love with the love you lavished upon me; fill my mind with your wisdom; place within these arms your perfect strength. And someday, when we stand in your radiant presence—this child and I—may we bask in your loving smile, two pleasing and complete masterpieces of your workmanship, two children returned home forever. Amen.

NOTES

Introduction: Lost in a Strange New World

1. C. Wright Mills, "The Post-Modern Family," cited at www.unu.edu/unupress/unupbooks/uu13se/uu13se03.htm.
2. Edward Shorter, *The Making of the Modern Family* (New York: Basic Books, 1975).

Chapter 2: Beginning with Love

1. Henry Drummond, *The Greatest Thing in the World* (Chicago, New York: Fleming H. Revell, 1890).
2. Erich Fromm, *The Art of Loving* (New York: Harper, 1956).
3. Sydney J. Harris, quoted in Glenn van Exeren, ed., *Speaker's Sourcebook II: Quotes, Stories, and Anecdotes for Every Occasion* (Englewood Cliffs, NJ: Prentice Hall, 1994).
4. Research from University of Miami School of Medicine's Touch Research Institute, cited in Tom McNichol, "The Power of Touch," *USA Weekend*, February 6–8, 1998.
5. Ibid.
6. Ibid.
7. Marcelene Cox, quoted in www.worldofquotes.com/topic/children-_-youth.
8. Charles E. Hummel, *Freedom from Tyranny of the Urgent* (New York: InterVarsity, 1997).

Notes

Chapter 4: The Power of Protection

1. "How Honest Are You?" in *Reader's Digest,* January 2004.
2. Lewis Smedes, "The Power of Promises," in *A Chorus of Witnesses,* ed. Thomas G. Long and Cornelius Plantinga Jr. (Grand Rapids, MI: Eerdmans, 1994.
3. *The Brown University Child and Adolescent Behavior Letter,* vol. 18, no. 4 (April 2002).

Chapter 5: Defusing the Anger Explosion

1. Alan Beck, Souris, Prince Edward Island, Canada, quoted in http://www.preachingtoday.com.

Chapter 6: Confronting the Media Monster

1. *Newsweek,* July 20, 1992.
2. Maggie Fox, "Just Hour of TV a Day Leads to Violence, Study Says," ABCNEWS.com (March 28, 2002).
3. Lisa McLaughlin, "R-Rated Behavior," *Time,* February 25, 2002.
4. Newton Minow, Speech to the National Association of Broadcasters on May 9, 1961; reprinted in *Chicago Tribune,* April 24, 2001.
5. Ibid.
6. Thomas Hazlett, "Requiem for the V-Chip," posted at http://slate.msn.com, February 13, 2004.

Chapter 7: Nurturing Young Spirits

1. "Introducing Christ to Your Child," *Preaching Today,* tape no. 92, cited at http://www.preachingtoday.com.
2. Rachel K. Sobel, "The Mysteries of Hope and Healing," *U.S. News and World Report,* January 26, 2004.

Chapter 8: Coping with Fear, Anxiety, and Depression

1. Marilyn Elias, "Childhood Depression," *USA Today,* August 13, 1998, 2D.

Chapter 11: Parting Words

1. George Barna, "Inward, Outward, and Upward: Ministry That Transforms Lives," report of the Barna Research Group (Ventura, CA, 1999), 18–23.

ABOUT THE AUTHOR

Ross Campbell, M.D., has spent over thirty years as a clinical psychiatrist, concentrating on the parent-child relationship. Formerly an associate clinical professor of pediatrics and psychiatry at the University of Tennessee College of Medicine, he is the author of the bestseller *How to Really Love Your Child*. Dr. Campbell has counseled thousands of parents throughout his extensive career and today writes and lectures on parenting topics.